Jewels of Cambodia

'The story of how the Christian church survived the horrors of the Killing Fields and has grown since is an inspiring one. It is a story in which World Vision has been privileged to play a key role. I have met several of the people Brenda talks of in her book and like her have been deeply impressed with their testimony and commitment. This is a story that needs to be told and Brenda has done the world church a significant service by telling it.'
Peter Scott, World Vision UK

'In the natural world jewels are formed under intense heat and often obtained at high cost, Cambodian Jewels for the Kingdom of God, formed under the intense heat of persecution have been mined by many at high personal cost. This book records their story. A good read.'
Rev Dr Rob Frost

'A very stimulating read. An enthralling tale of what is happening in Cambodia today. Full of real people who jump out at you from the pages. A testimony to what God is doing now.'
Dr Peter Brierley, Christian Research

'Brenda paints pictures of these "jewels", both Cambodian's by birth and foreigners, privileged to serve God in difficult and often dangerous times. They mirror my own recollections and experience. Their stories deserve to be told as a testimony of how God can work despite the strongest opposition from Satan. It is a great encouragement to me to see, in print, so many of the achievements that have been made through the work. I feel blessed to hear stories of people's lives being changed as they have been brought into relationship with Christ. This has happened not only through our work but also through that of our colleagues in other mission agencies and, most of all, through the labours of the Cambodian Christians who are the real "Jewels of Cambodia".'
Geoff Collett, SAO Cambodia

'Informative and inspirational. This book will move you emotionally and challenge you spiritually.'
Dr Derek Stringer, National Director and Bible Teacher, Good News Broadcasting

'Over recent years Cambodia has tended to recede in the minds of the UK Christian public. There are new horrors and world shattering events to take up our attention. Brenda's latest book comes as a timely reminder that we need to continue to keep Cambodia on our spiritual radar.

In a very readable way Brenda blends the faith testimonies of missionaries and national believers with the continuing challenge of Cambodia's pain and spiritual need. We learn that it is the active faith and sacrifice of Christian workers that has enabled a dynamic and committed Cambodian church to rise from the ashes of man's inhumanity to man.

Reading this book will be a blessing and challenge to us all.'
Stewart Moulds, WEC International

Jewels of Cambodia

Brenda Sloggett

Authentic

11 10 09 08 07 06 05   7 6 5 4 3 2 1

First published 2005 by Authentic Media
9 Holdom Avenue, Bletchley, Milton Keynes, Bucks, MK1 1QR, UK
and 129 Mobilization Drive, Waynesboro, GA 30830-4575, USA
www.authenticmedia.co.uk

British Library Cataloguing in Publication Data
A catalogue record for this book is available from the British Library

ISBN 1-85078-637-2

Cover design by Robert Cox
Cover photo by Nigel Goddard
Typeset by Temple Design
Print Management by Adare Carwin

CONTENTS

PREFACE

I am writing this preface after the terrible Asian tsunami and many are asking, 'Where is God in all this?' There are no simple answers but I have personally witnessed some of the wonderful things God has wrought through the devastation and dreadful years of the Khmer Rouge in Cambodia when an estimated 1.2 million died. Our God is so great, so full of compassion and love, especially for people suffering from traumas and bereavement, that in such circumstances he can redeem those experiences and create beautiful jewels out of the suffering.

I could not have written this book without the prayerful and practical support of God's people. During my month's stay in Cambodia researching these stories I was constantly amazed at the details of God's provision and care in the way he arranged my schedule. I am indebted to Agnes Verner who kept me supplied with her 'special bug-free water' and beautiful fresh flowers in my room. Barnabas Mam's church gave me a moving welcome and I cherish the memories of the numbers of the congregation who queued up to speak to me after the service. When I flew to Siem Reap, Sokreaksa Himm met me at the airport and took great care of me throughout my stay.

The churches I attended during that month were vibrant, growing, warm gatherings of people, some of whom had survived the Killing Fields era but had suffered appalling tragedies during the war years. The power of God to redeem, heal and bind up the wounds of the broken-hearted could be seen in those congregations and the joy of the Lord that filled their services. It is my prayer that the survivors of the tsunami disaster will come to know our Saviour God in all their distress.

Stewart and Jean Moulds prompted me to write this book and their encouragement and prayer support has been invaluable. Brian Maher gave me access to some of his writings and went to great lengths to help me during my month's stay in Cambodia.

Finally I owe a debt of gratitude to Ivor Greer for the help he gave me through the two years I was writing. I am not good at the computer and he spent two nights at our home putting the manuscript into better shape and checking some of the facts. While I was writing the final chapters I was diagnosed with cancer and had to face major surgery. Ivor telephoned me early one morning when I was feeling very depressed. He quoted some beautiful scriptures and helped me to face the daunting prospect. He arranged for me to stay in the peaceful beauty of Bawtry Hall just before the surgery and kept my mind focused on the manuscript!

The faithful prayers of my friends in Cambodia and elsewhere have been heard and answered as I am making a good recovery but I realise how urgent are the times in which we live. Christ is coming again so let us all remember that great event and use every opportunity to spread the healing message of salvation.

Brenda Sloggett
January 2005

FOREWORD

Very few people know much about South East Asia in general or Cambodia in particular. Most of us have vague memories of news stories but little understanding of the day-to-day life of ordinary people in this distant part of the world. The recollections we do have are usually uncomfortable! This deeply turbulent region (which first drew the description 'Killing Fields') has seen genocide and persecution of minorities on a large scale. It is associated with cruel brutality and a distinct absence of the personal freedoms we take for granted in the West.

But this is far from the whole story. Brenda Sloggett has done us a great service in recounting her personal contact with this beautiful, but troubled, part of the world. Her story is full of unique insights and first-hand observations from her travels. While she does not shy away from describing difficulties the book is shot through with elements of hope and life. In this apparently arid and spiritually unlikely soil the green shoots of Christian faith are pushing through. On these pages we learn about the indigenous church through the eyes of local Christian believers. These women and men of faith face the same pressures which we face as Christians, with all the added problems of a culture which is antagonistic to Christianity.

It is my prayer that this book informs, educates and excites many of us who would otherwise be ignorant about this part of God's world. It is also my prayer that it encourages prayer support for those who share our faith and our destiny, but in much more difficult circumstances.

Stephen Gaukroger

CHAPTER ONE:

A Personal Perspective

Cambodia is a country that is little known to the western world, yet its scenery and culture captivates the first-time visitor. The tranquil beauty of the countryside creates an impression that time has stood still in this land of vibrant green rice paddies interspersed with picturesque settlements of bamboo and thatch houses. Sandwiched between Thailand and Vietnam, Cambodia is a land of great contrasts. The capital city of Phnom Penh has some stunning white temples, wide tree-lined boulevards, open parklands, houses built in French-style architecture and colourful street markets. The royal palace – a magnificent building with beautifully kept gardens – is perhaps its crowning glory.

Many main roads through Phnom Penh are in good condition but you can very quickly find roads not made up or with refuse-filled pot-holes, chickens and pigs scavenging for some scraps to eat, appalling slums and poverty-stricken homes with thin, poorly clad children playing with stones in the dust.

It was a TV documentary by John Pilger in 1979 that motivated me to take up the challenge to be involved with Cambodia. Its history is far from peaceful and it has been a country that was hard and unresponsive to the Christian message despite the pioneering work of two American Christian and Missionary Alliance (CAMA) couples, David

Even pigs scavenge for food

and Muriel Ellison and Arthur and Esther Hammond, who entered Cambodia in 1923. They were told, 'The Cambodians are staunch Buddhists, you cannot expect to have any success.' The Hammonds stayed in Phnom Penh, while the Ellisons went 200 miles north to Battambang, Cambodia's second city, where they established a small street chapel. By 1940 Arthur Hammond had completed his translation of the Bible but there was only a small response to the gospel message.

John Pilger's documentary showed the once beautiful capital city deserted; bomb damaged buildings, a bridge over the Bassac River had been blown up and an air of absolute dejection filled the viewer as scenes of the war-ravaged years were shown. The countryside had been turned into a vast slave labour camp and there were mass graves in the place of the vibrant green rice paddies. It showed the refugee camps of Thailand with thousands of homeless and destitute Cambodians who had fled the horrors of their homeland. Some of them died of disease or malnutrition when they reached the camps too late; others who survived were being resettled into western countries, and some so longed to be in their homeland that they waited patiently for the time when it was safe to return. It will help to understand why this tragedy happened if we learn a little of the history that preceded this event.

In 1953 when Cambodia was granted independence from France, some Khmer intellectuals had been studying in French universities where they converted to extreme Marxist political philosophy. One of these revolutionaries was Pol Pot. In 1965 all American Protestant missionaries were forced to leave Cambodia as a result of Prince Sihanouk's anti-American policies. The church had a membership at that time of less than a thousand believers. By 1970 Vietnamese communist forces joined with the Khmer communists (Khmer Rouge) under the leadership of Pol Pot and a terrible fear of what the future held gripped the nation.

Under the threat of war, a revival began to take place and hundreds of house churches sprang up almost overnight with some amazing stories of miraculous healings and evil spirits being driven out; hundreds from the student population turned to the Christian faith and began to evangelise. All this was augmented by a big crusade led by World Vision director, Dr Stanley Mooneyham. The crusade produced hundreds of new converts; many of them died during the Killing Fields era but Barnabas Mam and Paul, who later became known as 'Paul of Cambodia', survived and went on to fulfil a significant role in the growth of the church. Chhirc Taing was the country's Christian leader. He came to Britain to take a postgraduate degree in engineering at Heriot Watt University in Edinburgh. While staying in Scotland he met Paul and Helen Penfold and they shared his love for the land of Cambodia. He attended the Keswick Convention in 1973 and gave an impassioned plea from the platform for prayer for his homeland. In the UK Cambodia for Christ (later to become SAO Cambodia) was formed. As the political situation in Cambodia worsened Chhirc felt he must return home to be with the Cambodian church. His plea for prayer met with remarkable answers in Cambodia. A revival was taking place and Overseas Missionary Fellowship sent in a team of five missionaries. As the gospel message spread and grew miraculously against a backcloth of war and bombing, the capital city filled with refugees from the provinces where the Khmer Rouge had begun their regime of genocide.

In 1975 Phnom Penh was surrounded by Khmer Rouge forces and completely cut off except by air. A massive airlift of key diplomats and other important people took place with air drops of supplies which kept the population in the besieged city alive until April that same year, when the Americans pulled out. When all the missionaries made a reluctant exodus, the total number of Christians stood at around ten thousand. Between 1975 and 1979 Cambodia was changed into one vast slave labour camp, when an estimated more than two million people died and hundreds of thousands of survivors fled to the refugee camps of Thailand.

The death and destruction affected virtually all the Khmer Christian leaders and 90 per cent of the church. This included Chhirc Taing who died in 1975 – martyred for his faith; Barnabas Mam was arrested and taken to a slave labour camp, and Paul, who remained in the city in a variety of secret venues and in great fear met with the few remaining Christians. It was the darkest hour of Cambodia's history, yet through these terrible events God was turning the evil machinations of humanity into an era of hope when the glorious message of the gospel would be spread throughout the land in a way no one could ever have envisaged.

After I had watched the 1979 Pilger documentary I felt motivated to contribute in some way to help the Cambodian refugees in Thailand. I had no idea how I could be involved so over a period of six months I asked the Lord to direct me to a Christian mission that was helping this land. Through my husband's involvement with Gideon's International I was introduced to Southeast Asian Outreach (now known as SAO Cambodia) and began to help with refugees coming to this country. Paul and Helen Penfold, together with Chhirc Taing, founded SAO Cambodia in 1973. They asked if we could provide a home for two Cambodian girls who had arrived at their Cambodian Refugee Centre in Gravesend. John and Valerie Heard were involved with this centre which was a safe haven for these traumatised people who had arrived in England. I shall never forget the day John and Valerie introduced us to our Cambodian girls and we welcomed them into their new home. Thida and Bhoppa looked around their freshly furnished flat with amazement and we just loved them both immediately.

The girls were brought up in the capital city; their father being a silk merchant ensured a good education. In 1975 their secure home and family life was interrupted dramatically very early in the morning when they were still in their beds. They were in their early teens when they heard loud speakers ordering everyone to leave their homes as the Americans were coming. They were told it was only for three days and then they could return. Their parents collected the grandparents and loaded enough food and changes of clothing for three days into the car. There was no space for Thida and Bhoppa so they walked behind the car that drove slowly into a mass exodus of all the city dwellers. The scene in front of them was shocking: families with babies, old people scarcely able to walk, children crying in fright and even some patients from the hospitals being pushed along in their beds! Thankfully, it was the dry season so the ground was rock hard but the scorching overhead sun caused several to collapse through lack of water. In the rear were young teenage trained Khmer Rouge soldiers who shouted at everyone to keep moving.

The first night their car was confiscated by the soldiers so all of them had to continue on foot. They slept that night on the roadside from sheer exhaustion. After a month of walking the monsoon rains began to fall and the roadsides were awash with mud. Sometimes they managed to find somewhere to rest at night, under the bamboo-thatch houses of villagers whose homes are built on stilts to keep out the snakes. Sharing the space with chickens and pigs, they slept little as they were frequently cold, wet and hungry as their food supply had run out. Other nights were spent on the roadside with no protection from the malarial mosquitoes that hummed overhead. They drank from puddles and were forced to continue the endless walking.

The soldiers split the family up and classified their grandparents as part of the 'old people' but Thida and Bhoppa were listed as 'new people'. They needed to be re-educated in the harsh communistic teachings that all were equal and they must work hard all day and half the night if they wished to survive. The girls lost track of the rest of their family and were given a space on the floor of a commune shelter that was only a thatch roof supported by wooden posts, with no walls. During the night it leaked water from the rains and they were woken at the crack of dawn by loud whistles blown by the soldiers ordering them to work without breakfast, shovelling heavy spade-loads of earth to create a dam.

Thida and Bhoppa had spent their time in Phnom Penh making beautiful silk dresses. Unaccustomed to such heavy work they were frequently exhausted and at the point of starvation. If anyone was unable to complete their work quota they were lined up at the end of the day and bludgeoned to death. In the evenings they had to listen to harsh shouting from the soldiers to obey their orders and work harder. Each morning they observed people missing from their group but fear dominated their lives and no one dared to ask questions. One morning they were taken to the Mekong riverside and boarded a boat which took them downstream to another part of the countryside. Malaria, dysentery and starvation killed many of the slave labourers but Thida and Bhoppa managed to survive in these terrible conditions. Bhoppa went down with a bad bout of malaria so Thida searched for a special tropical flower which they crushed in water and drank to keep her fever low. There was no access to any health care.

Daily they saw people dying from disease, exhaustion, and towards the end of the day they had to watch the soldiers shoot anyone who had disobeyed their orders. Some of the slave labourers were forced to dig a mass grave and Thida and Bhoppa were ordered to fill the grave after they witnessed some of the people were being buried alive. Knowing they could not survive long in these horrible conditions they escaped from the commune one night and hid in the forest areas as they made their way to the Vietnamese border. They had a relative who lived in Vietnam who was able to make contact with an uncle in Hong Kong, but Vietnamese soldiers found them and ordered them into a camp for deserters. Conditions in this camp were as bad as those under the Khmer Rouge. Despite their weak state they made a decision to leave the camp during the night and walk to the Thai border and find a refugee camp.

On the long, hazardous journey they bartered their gold earrings for rice and managed to find their way through mined fields. They had spent four years living in fear and famine so when a Red Cross bus appeared in the distance they felt elation that at last they were leaving the horrors of Cambodia behind. The Red Cross took them to the Khao Dang refugee camp where they lived for nine months. They constructed a simple bamboo-thatch hut and lived on a daily ration of rice, tinned fish and a few vegetables. Finally they were transferred to a transit camp for health checks and were given refugee status to come to England. As they travelled in the coach which took them to Bangkok airport, a huge surge of relief swept over them that the horrors of Cambodia, their homeland, was now past history.

Thida and Bhoppa settled in well to a new life in the freedom of England but they still had the memories that had travelled with them during those awful years. We sent them to college to learn English and they were soon at the top of the class. Both of them wanted to learn tailoring, English style, so they attended classes at college to help them work with wool fabrics. Their tutor soon told me that their own skills were more than adequate so they happily set up their own dressmaking business and I was able to watch them gradually adapt to our different way of life. At that time I observed how easily their dark eyes dimmed with unshed tears but they were determined to make a success of their new life. It was not until I had visited their country that I fully realised what a huge difference of culture, weather and lifestyle they had to face.

Their courage and gentle, sweet smiles when they came to our house endeared them to our family and when my daughter married they made the most beautiful wedding gown and bridesmaids' dresses. Thida and Bhoppa moved to London five years later but we kept in touch and they visited us frequently. In 1985 Thida met Meng and we had the joy of attending the wedding. Bhoppa made a visit to the States to see her grandmother who had been found and resettled there. In 1990 she met and married an American Cambodian and settled in Philadelphia.

In 1991 I made my first visit to Cambodia as a voluntary worker with World Vision. As the plane from Saigon, Vietnam landed at Pochentong airport I felt a deep sense of gratitude to my heavenly Father for allowing me to see this land that I had learnt much about during the years when we helped the refugees that were resettled in England. A taxi took me from the airport to the capital city Phnom Penh and en route I was fascinated by the scenery. The city had a distinctive charm with its wide tree-lined boulevards, a few parks and some stunning temples. Many of the roads were lined with flame trees and fragrant frangipani.

As a first-time visitor to Phnom Penh I was charmed by its beauty, shocked by its poverty, frightened by its traffic, amazed at its diversity and deeply disturbed by the amputees sitting on the pavements begging. These are the legacy of the terrible war years when thousands or perhaps more accurately millions of merciless landmines were indiscriminately planted throughout the country. Manufactured in the west they provided a handsome income for these wealthy countries. To our shame no one has been able to totally ban the manufacture of these terrible weapons.

During this visit I saw some of the awful vestiges of the war years; mass graves, a monument filled with skulls, children dying from malnutrition, derelict buildings, refuse on every street and a general air of hopelessness. Before I left England people asked me, 'Does the money we give really get there? If so what difference does it make?' When a country has been embroiled in war for nearly 20 years, its infrastructure wrecked, over two million of its own people brutally killed because they were educated, vast areas of land rendered useless for cultivation due to landmines; the road to recovery cannot be short term.

Over the past ten years I have made several short visits to Cambodia and have had the privilege of meeting some of the 'Jewels of Cambodia' who have made significant changes to this land and helped to ignite the dying embers of the decimated church. My contacts have been largely through SAO Cambodia, World Vision, WEC International and friends of the people who have worked for these organisations. This is, of necessity, a personal account of the Cambodian church from my observations. It, by no means, gives an exhaustive or comprehensive picture but I hope it will, by God's grace, serve to inform and challenge many to pray more effectively for this land.

CHAPTER TWO:

Verners:
through Thailand to Cambodia

During my initial visit to Cambodia in 1991, I had visited the National Paediatric Hospital which was built and funded by World Vision. The desperate needs of the country were evidenced in this being the only children's hospital in the country at that time. World Vision had been helping Cambodia for many years and they lost some of their valuable workers during the Pol Pot years. The hospital was beautifully run but a tour of the wards with the World Vision Director left me in a state of shock. There were wards of extremely sick children suffering from TB, meningitis and dengue fever but the most shocking wards for me, were those with children suffering from severe malnutrition. Many of those children were dying as they had reached the hospital far too late. I thought of the vast quantities of food we eat in the west where obesity is a problem, and sadly some never give a thought to the starving peoples of the world.

In October 1991 the Paris Peace Accords were signed. This resulted in the formation of an interim Supreme National Council in Phnom Penh, headed by Prince Sihanouk and the deployment of the United Nations Transitional Authority in Cambodia (UNTAC) with 22,000 peace-keepers to disarm the warring factions and organise elections. This was a necessary force but the presence of these soldiers had significant effects on the country, both economically (with rents escalating) and socially (with more demand for prostitution).

The Khmer Rouge were still a threat to the peace process. Cambodia during the early nineties was a volatile place to live with frequent gun fights and armed robberies. Christians who went to help needed to have a definite calling and to recognise that helping this land and its traumatised people would be a costly enterprise. Despite the dangers, progress was being made and the Phnom Penh Bible School was established and a team of translators under the auspices of the United Bible Society began working on a new translation of the Bible.

SAO Cambodia gained entrance to Cambodia with projects of fish farming and eye health care, and their vision was to bring the message of salvation to the people through these projects representing the Bread of Life and the Light of the World. In 1993 I joined the SAO Council and made my next visit to Cambodia the same year. It was the first year of real hope for Cambodia as refugees from the camps returned to Cambodia to vote in their first 'democratic' elections. The Khmer Rouge still existed as a constant threat to peace and there was no clear winner in the elections. A coalition was formed with Prince Rannaridh and Hun Sen as co-prime ministers.

The Reverend Jim and Mrs Agnes Verner, WEC missionaries seconded to SAO, met me at the airport. I had heard all about them but this was my first meeting and I was immediately drawn to them with their warm welcome. Worldwide Evangelisation for Christ (WEC) is a mission founded by C.T. Studd, the famous cricketer who responded to God's call to take the message of salvation to China and later on to Africa. In 1993, there was no opening for WEC missionaries to work directly with the church so

Revd Jim and Mrs Agnes Verner

the Verners arrived in Cambodia as Field Directors for SAO Cambodia.

But their journey to Cambodia was one of long waiting and preparation. When Jim trained for service with WEC in 1965, he believed God had called him to Cambodia. Waiting for the door to open in Cambodia he started his missionary career in Thailand, and it was there he met Agnes, a Canadian WEC missionary who became his wife. A music teacher, language supervisor and violinist, Agnes radiates the love of Christ, so with her natural beauty it is no wonder Jim fell in love. When the Vietnam War and the Pol Pot terrors closed the door to Cambodia, both continued to work tirelessly in neighbouring Thailand.

They pioneered an entirely new work in Sukhothai Province which had a reputation for bandits, violence and robberies. God richly blessed this work by changing the lives of opium addicts, spirit worshippers and spirit mediums. They arrived in Thailand in 1965 and found Thailand economically poor, with lawlessness, thugs, and bands of robbers roaming the countryside rustling domestic water buffalo: life was dangerous and difficult. They were expecting their mission to be hard and costly so they settled into a very basic house and began language study. A Thai believer called Lambuen taught them the culture and much about the animistic beliefs.

In 1968 a real revival broke out and lasted until 1972. Drug addicts were converted and signs and wonders took place. Their animist friends believed in the supernatural and they saw people healed instantly of TB.

One morning, Jim and Agnes had a special time of prayer when God gave them a word of prophecy warning them of dangers and telling them to ask for protection. The arranged meetings took place and all were blessed with much encouragement but on the journey back home problems surfaced. The access road was strewn with thorn bushes and the church elder who was riding the motorbike with Jim shouted in his ear, 'It's a trap! Speed for the forest and we will meet up on the main road.' He did just that and as the church elder jumped off the bike it distracted the bandits who were lying in wait to steal the bike.

Jim and Agnes had a series of raids when many of their personal possessions were stolen. The church elder sent a message to the bandit leader telling him to stop attacking the Verners as Buddha would not want them harmed! Small groups of believers were formed in homes and they rapidly grew in the faith and began to develop spiritual gifts so the Verners were able to place the suitable believers into places of leadership. They visited these small churches weekly to teach and encourage but after feeling really exhausted with their heavy schedule they were delighted when one of the elders of these churches agreed to do some of their work. Constantly under attack from opposition they were often tired and lonely but other members of the WEC team stood by them in prayer. Then they heard the faithful elder had been shot and killed by the bandits as he rode Jim's bike. The robber clearly had intended to kill Jim. The Verners shed tears for this much loved man and laid his body to rest in the village he had served.

> Those who sow in tears will reap with songs of joy.
> He who goes out weeping,
> carrying seed to sow,
> will return with songs of joy. (Ps. 126:5,6)

As they reflected over this sad incident they little thought that they would face another murder in their ministry. But this tragedy had a dramatic effect on the other villagers. A revival began that lasted four years but it ran alongside hardships, tears, weariness and constant vigilance against robbers. After losing one motorbike they decided to use push bikes and covered a lot of miles in this manner. But this was not plain sailing because Jim was riding a bike alongside a Thai brother when a petrol tanker swerved to avoid a vehicle on the busy, congested road. As it swerved it hit Jim, throwing him ten metres into the air. He fell unconscious on the ground and an ambulance was called. Agnes hastened to the scene with an elderly Thai believer who was living with them. Granny Rawady was a woman of faith and she said loudly: 'This is not unto death. You people will receive news from Bangkok inside ten days that Jim has begun to recover.'

Jim was unconscious on a drip for exactly ten days. He woke up and asked the nurses for his favourite Thai curry! Agnes who had stayed by his bedside sent the news to Granny Rawady that her word had come true. Jim subsequently caught typhus from an infected blood transfusion but in God's goodness made a complete recovery. The Verners were elected into field leadership and were involved in setting up the Evangelical Fellowship of Thailand. In 1993 there were many churches functioning on a self-supporting basis throughout the country including 63 which had grown from the work of WEC. The Thai believers chose to call them 'Bonds of Fellowship'. The work had been hard, exhausting, exhilarating and encouraging but as they watched all the events that were taking place in neighbouring Cambodia they began studying the Khmer language and prayed daily that God would open the door for them to enter the land they had been commissioned to go to 28 years earlier. The years spent in Thailand were clearly used by God to train and prepare the Verners for their work and calling to Cambodia.

In 1985 one of the churches that the Verners had planted in Thailand was a place of refuge for Barnabas Mam when he fled from the communists in Cambodia. Sick, starving and in great fear, he was ministered to by these believers in a loving way. (It was several years later before they knew of this from Barnabas himself after he returned to Phnom Penh.) The believers hid Barnabas from the Thai police who captured him later and put him in prison; but this divine intervention showed how God was in control and how deeply he cared for this man. Being fed and cared for lovingly gave him the strength to continue his journey to Site Two camp where he found his wife and children.

During my second visit to Phnom Penh in 1993 I saw drab, unkempt school buildings that had long since been abandoned; naked, dirty children played near garbage piles stacked at street corners; pigs and scavenging dogs, who roamed the city in packs, competing together for some scraps of food to eat. There was an overall smell of refuse and decay which gave rise to feelings of helplessness in having so little to give to so many. It was clear that the hope of seeing changes would take years of hard, exhausting work, long periods with little time off, intercessory prayer meetings, and pleading day and night to our loving compassionate God for strength to get through each day.

At that time of uncertainty the church was meeting discreetly and everything was kept 'low key'. Mission personnel unobtrusively attended house meetings and it was at one of these that the Verners met Paul, who was later to become known as Paul of Cambodia. While they were able to have times of fellowship, they had to exercise care – changing the venue, arriving and leaving in a variety of different ways – which helped to avoid publicising their activities. Expatriates held a weekly prayer time for the church. There were probably about 300 believers attending small groups in the city at that time, and there was a witness, however weak, in 20 of the 22 provinces. The government gave official recognition to the Christian Church in April 1990 and this was celebrated on April 6th in a big open meeting in Phnom Penh. But this agreement was largely unknown in the provinces and there was still persecution of Christians from the Khmer Rouge soldiers, and also some Buddhist monks saw anyone who converted to Christianity as a renegade who must be shunned.

It was distressing to see orphaned children on the streets begging for food; so many men had been killed in the war that the remaining widows also joined the beggars, as they had no assistance from anyone. At night the sounds of warring factions could be heard. Many carried guns; lawlessness, burglaries and theft of vehicles was rampant between 1993 and 1996. Corruption was rife everywhere.

In 1993, when the elections took place under the control of UNTAC, refugees were able to leave the camps in Thailand and elsewhere and vote in the elections. The economic and social effects of UNTAC were being felt in

Cambodia. High rents made it difficult for those on slender budgets to make ends meet; pornography, trashy western culture, HIV, AIDS arrived with a vengeance. There was no clear winner in the elections but FUNCIPEC (The Royalist Party) led by Prince Rannaridh, one of the sons of Sihanouk won the most seats. The Cambodian People's Party (CPP) of Hun Sen which had been the incumbent party in Phnom Penh was a close second so a coalition was formed with Hun Sen and Prince Rannaridh as co-prime ministers. But there was still political turmoil. UNTAC went home but left behind an emerging AIDS pandemic and thousands of unwanted mixed race babies, filling orphanages with babies that most Cambodians were not interested in adopting.

As I went with Jim and Agnes Verner to see some of the SAO projects they told me how they felt after seeing all the needs in this land. Agnes told me of a vision she had one night of a spectre from hell looming before her. She shared it with Jim and they spent the rest of the night in intercessory prayer for the nation, the church and the Christians who had come to help these appalling conditions. The next day, travelling on the back of a hired motordop (a local motorbike taxi), they saw the most pathetic sight they had ever encountered: a girl of between fourteen and sixteen, crippled and crawling through the monsoon-filled swamps by the roadside was dragging a plastic sheet on which lay a newborn baby. They were helpless to assist as they had been called out to another emergency that was also life-threatening, but that awful scene haunted Agnes for a long time. When they received a donated Land Rover they were able to assist many more desperate people.

Soon, however, Christian medical services and development agencies began to tackle the terrible plight of the destitute within the city and in the provinces, and literally worked day and night to build up the badly needed infrastructure: sewage, clean water, lighting, homes for the homeless, hospitals, justice, human rights, and the list goes on… the darkness gave way to the light of hope which glowed in the countless faces of smiling believers. The incomparable Light of the World and the Bread of Life began to shine in the darkness and the once decimated church began to grow.

Only two of the seven churches in Revelation chapters 2 and 3 have survived to the present day; Smyrna and Philadelphia. They were suffering churches that remained loyal to Christ even to death. 'I know your afflictions and your poverty – yet you are rich', was said 2,000 years ago to Symrna (see Rev. 2:9). The same words of comfort could be said to the church of Cambodia today. It was formed in darkness but in a coming Day will shine with radiance as part of the bride of Christ: 'its brilliance was like that of a very precious jewel, like jasper, clear as crystal' (Rev. 21:11).

CHAPTER THREE:

The Goddards
and other Restoration Workers

During those early years it was difficult to establish which need was the uppermost. SAO Cambodia's vision to bring Christ as the Bread of Life through their fish farming projects and the Light of the World through their eye health care work was a great step forward in very needy areas. There were many people who were blind and all they needed was a cataract operation so SAO had skilled ophthalmologists performing these operations in a refurbished ward in one of the hospitals in Phnom Penh. As there were many refugees returning to their homeland with no possessions or the skills to earn a living, a handicraft project to teach art and jewellery was also set up in Phnom Penh. All these projects had a vision to share the gospel in an appropriate way, and God has blessed this ministry as accompanying the workers were experienced missionaries Jim and Agnes Verner. A School of Optometry was established, the first of its kind in Phnom Penh. Today it is entirely run by trained Khmer staff.

In the rural areas malnutrition was a major problem; lack of educated people led to a vacuum of knowledge in how to tackle the enormous deficiencies that existed in every level of society. The villages had no resources and the children were half their normal size and often had light red hair; a symptom of vitamin deficiency. SAO Cambodia sent highly qualified aquaculturalists Nigel Goddard from Weybridge and Milet Santos from the Philippines to reintroduce fish farms to help this situation. Milet took me with her to visit one of the villages where she had set up a fish farm project and also helped the people to grow vegetables.

Milet had grown up in the Philippines but had some difficult years in her twenties when both her parents died prematurely. She had a brother and two sisters who were younger than her and, determined to support her orphaned brother and sisters, she used her considerable intellect to win scholarships and finally obtained a doctorate in aquaculture. She was motivated to help others who had suffered and through these experiences God had shown her his sufficiency as her heavenly Father. She believed God wanted her to realise that she could be his hands to touch hurting, wounded and broken people in Cambodia.

On my second visit, I accompanied Milet and Nigel to see the large Aquaculture Centre that had been built by SAO Cambodia in a village about an hour's drive from the city. It was a bumpy ride over the pot-holed dirt roads. Nigel made a commitment to Christ in his twenties and then qualified in aquaculture and applied to Voluntary Service Overseas (VSO) seeking to get some practical experience in working in poor countries. He was successful in the selection procedure but at the same time he heard of the SAO Cambodia Aquaculture Programme. God's timing was perfect; he enabled a partnership to be formed between VSO and SAO. This was a real confirmation that God had chosen Cambodia for him to use his professional skills and with his love for Christ he wanted to spread the message of salvation in this needy place.

Jim and Agnes Verner went with us to visit the village near the Aquaculture Centre as they were going to their weekly outreach work in the poor villages. We arrived and as soon as we climbed out of the vehicle, children from the village ran to greet us and sat on the dusty ground to hear Bible stories from Milet and Agnes. These shabbily dressed little dark-eyed children were enthralled by the stories, and sat perfectly still with rapt attention. Later their parents came and Jim began to preach the good news with large coloured pictures that illustrated the stories he told to the village people. The Verners with Nigel and Milet had built bridges of friendship in helping with the physical needs of the people. With no access to medical care Agnes prayed for them in their sickness and saw miracles of healing. Sometimes a child needing urgent treatment would be taken to a hospital in Phnom Penh.

The introduction of fish farms, providing the necessary additional nutrition to meagre diets was a good way of bringing Jesus as the Bread of Life to these people. With their professional skills they were able to introduce fish into the ponds that fed on the available waste in each particular village; termites were a nuisance in one, so termite-eating fish were introduced. Another village had ducks, so fish that fed on duck droppings were put into the ponds to breed. In the Aquaculture Centre were the tanks that hatched the fingerlings of all these different types of fish. At that time a small church began to grow from this ministry.

There were other SAO Cambodia members who contributed to this ministry: one being Mary, a Khmer convert, who was particularly talented in teaching the children in the Saturday school. Using Khmer children's songs and teaching them colouring and painting, all the children enjoyed those special days. Mary tells her testimony:

I come from a non-Christian family; my parents are Chinese and Khmer and hold strict beliefs about religion. I heard the good news through a teacher at school. She explained about Jesus and lent me a Bible. I treated it as a storybook until I went through a troubled part of my life in having to earn enough money to support my family. Then as I prayed to God the living word came to me from John 16:33: 'I have told you these things, so that in me you may have peace. In this world you will have trouble. But take heart! I have overcome the world.' I read that same sentence over and over again and God has been true to his word and supplied all my need.

The appreciative parents of the children soon came along to hear Jim preach, and they listened with great interest. A New Testament in Khmer was given to the headman of the village. Before we left to walk to the next village, I watched the assembled crowd listening to the headman reading passages from the Bible under the shade of a coconut palm. We walked on rough ground alongside rice paddies to the next village, where more meetings were held. Agnes ministered to any medical needs and prayed for the sick. It was a long hot afternoon and the sun was beginning to go down when we wearily returned to the Land Cruiser that had taken us there. Just as I was getting in, a huge snake slithered across the road. I was so relieved it hadn't put in an appearance before we walked through those fields!

Evening shadows were falling and the sky turned from pink to red, followed by a golden glow that lit up the ponds with a pale lemon light, while the sugar palms changed to dark shades of green as the sky darkened. It was all so beautiful; it seemed hardly possible that the land on which the Aquaculture Centre had been built was once a dam made by slave labourers in the Pol Pot days. Mary was aware of this so when the outreach started at this place she prayed every day that God would do something special.

One night she had a dream in which she saw the Development Centre and the villages surrounding it. A large white dove flew over the whole area and built a nest in one of the trees bordering the centre. The whole area had been one great labour camp and it was here that Thida and Bhoppa worked from dawn to dusk and were forced to watch starving forced labourers end the day being shot or bludgeoned to death if they had not done their work quota.

Now these same people who had survived that era were listening to the wonderful message of forgiveness, healing and hope through the knowledge of the Saviour of the world. In the evening while I sat in my room in the city, I read chapters 3 and 4 of Malachi. Chapter 4 states, '"Surely the day is coming; it will burn like a furnace. All the arrogant and every evildoer will be stubble, and that day that is coming will set them on fire," says the LORD Almighty ... "But for you who revere my name, the sun of righteousness will arise with healing in [his] wings."' As the sun set over that rural area of Cambodia, I knew there was a sun rising with healing in his wings. The message of the Son of God, who gave his life to save the lost, was now being spread into that land and there would be a harvest of precious souls saved for eternal life.

These villagers had seen unspeakable horrors, lost loved ones during the terrible years, but now the Lord of the harvest was preparing their hearts to receive the message of grace and forgiveness, bringing healing to their wounded souls. The servants of God who ministered to these people, had themselves been prepared through dark and difficult times, refining their characters, giving them a radiance that reflected a facet of the beauty of their Master. The weekly outreach continued for six years and took place on the only day that team members had for relaxation. It was sacrificial serving but God is nobody's debtor.

Today there is a growing church in a separate building under the leadership of Pastor Cheam Vath. He came to Phnom Penh in 1991 as a cyclo driver where he met staff who were planning the aquaculture work right at the beginning of SAO's work in Cambodia. Vath was led to the Lord and baptised and began to work at the Aquaculture Centre.

In 1994 Nigel and Milet took over the aquaculture work. Sparks flew between them and frequently they did not see eye to eye. After some difficult situations they began to understand that they had to learn mutual respect for one another. They confided in Jim Verner who was instrumental in helping them to get on together. Eventually, through prayer and assurance that God was in control they began to see each other in a new light. They fell in love!

Milet attended a Bible study on one evening a week and Nigel took her to the house in the Land Cruiser and collected her afterwards. As he was returning to the vehicle one dark evening, two armed Khmer men sprang out of the darkness and held a gun to Nigel's chest. They said, 'Hand over the keys or you will be a dead man!' With such a threat, Nigel reluctantly handed over the keys. This was one of many similar incidents that took place daily in this turbulent country. Little did Nigel realise then that far worse problems would arise (as we will see later) which would test his stamina spiritually and that of Milet too.

Over a period of time, with wise counsel and a prophecy from a visiting missionary pastor they felt God confirming their relationship with each other. Milet needed one more assurance before finalising her commitment and that was to see if she could embrace Nigel's background and culture. She travelled to England, met Nigel's family, friends and church and returned to Cambodia without any reservations so they married in July 1995 and completed a study course

Nigel and Milet Goddard with Sion and Jasmine

at Redcliffe Bible College before returning to the project in May 1996. God was in this break as both of them had been through some very testing times in the city.

The timing of their marriage was clearly of the Lord and I had the pleasure of attending it at Weybridge, rejoicing with them in their joy. I had a special link with this couple as Milet's mother had only been fifty years old when Milet lost her and mine had been the same age. Nigel had completed part of his studies at the Ministry of Agriculture's Veterinary Laboratories in Weybridge where I had completed part of my studies in medical laboratory work too.

Politically the country was unstable because the Khmer Rouge forces had not been eliminated and fighting continued between the Royal Cambodian Armed Forces and Khmer Rouge troops in Battambang Province. Although de-mining programmes were in place there were hundreds of victims needing hospital treatment from exploding mines in the rural areas. The hospitals were appalling and many of the patients died of infections. Government officials thrived on bribery and corruption. Missions and aid organisations were helping in significant ways but sometimes it appeared as a drop in the bucket, as the country was also receiving an influx of returning refugees. These people had spent years in the camps and were driven by bus to Phnom Penh. Once back home they faced almost insurmountable problems.

CHAPTER FOUR:

A Visionary Jewel: Barnabas Mam

It was in 1993 that Jim and Agnes Verner introduced me to one of the returning refugees who was to make a huge impact on the growth of the church in Cambodia. Agnes drove me to the small street where Pastor Barnabas Mam and his wife Boury had been able to rent a flat. Barnabas greeted me with the warmest smile I had seen and Boury stood by his side obviously admiring her husband. I marvelled at the joy that both possessed despite all the trials they had endured.

Barnabas had been brought up in a Buddhist family, his father being well known as a traditional healer. Barnabas became a healer too; when he was seven years old and after junior high school he lived in a wat (a Buddhist pagoda) under the guardianship of an uncle and he became a Buddhist Master of Ceremonies at the age of eighteen. When all the threats of the communists taking over Cambodia gradually became a reality he joined the communist revolutionaries in 1970.

He was sent to a World Vision crusade in 1971 to spy on the event and be a troublemaker. The speaker was Dr Stanley Mooneyham and the message of the prodigal son touched his heart and he ended the evening by praying the sinner's prayer. His uncle and his father were very angry with him for leaving Buddhism and they removed all financial support. He soon learnt the cost of commitment to

Pastor Barnabas Mam

Christ but his conduct was so good that his relatives agreed his conversion was not such a big loss to their family. However, his friends in the communist movement regarded him as a traitor.

He joined the Bethany Church in Phnom Penh where he began to hear about a man called Chhirc Taing who was studying in the UK. He began to harbour resentment against this man whom he had never met but was held in such high esteem. In 1973, when Chhirc returned to Phnom Penh, the two men met and Barnabas was immediately won over by Chhirc's gracious Christ-likeness. Chhirc became the leader of the church and Barnabas was mentored by him.

He began to study English with a Christian and Missionary Alliance teacher and attended the International

Church where he listened attentively to their teachers, including a CAMA missionary called Norman Ens. Obtaining employment with World Vision, he saved what little he could to purchase his first Bible and met with the few believers in the underground church. He remembers the last meeting he had with Chhirc Taing on 16 April 1975 as the Khmer Rouge were just about to overrun Phnom Penh and the threat of death was a reality to all the Christians at that time. Chhirc told Barnabas to be faithful even to death and after sharing the Lord's Supper together, Chhirc left the house and was martyred shortly afterwards.

In 1975 Barnabas was captured by the Khmer Rouge and evacuated to the countryside along with thousands of others. Charged with being a servant of the American Imperialists he was brainwashed and forced to do hard labour for a year and a half. Constantly under the threat of death he kept the faith by singing, 'When the roll is called up yonder'. His captors found his smiling face and total composure unnerving, and they asked him where he found such beautiful music. There were times when he was too frightened to sing but the reality of his faith shone in the darkest places and his captors just could not bring themselves to kill him.

He was transferred to an area near Battambang where the Khmer Rouge gathered for a massacre of innocent Cambodians before they reached the Thai border. An order was given to the commander to kill all 300 relocated Cambodians together with Barnabas. This commander was alarmed at this situation as he knew the Khmer Rouge intended to kill every Khmer person and this edict was part of the programme. Barnabas was told that he would have to die so he replied that he knew where he was going because he knew Jesus as his Saviour, but then he asked the commander how he would feel about meeting God as his judge if he killed all these countrymen and women. The commander looked afraid and did not obey the orders. Instead the whole contingent escaped with the commander to the Tonle Sap lake where they stayed secretly for a month before returning to Phnom Penh. On the journey back to the city they witnessed the death of many Khmer Rouge cadres in retaliation by those they had repressed. Arriving in Phnom Penh, Barnabas organised the group to sign a petition that he presented to the government to spare the life of the Khmer Rouge commander. The petition was granted and the commander was given a home with a Christian pastor.

After Pol Pot, Barnabas had taken the long journey on foot back to Phnom Penh to find his family. It took two months; he was sick and starving and didn't have one proper meal. On the way he began to wonder exactly how old were his parents and whether he would ever see his brothers and sisters again. He met a cousin on a bridge and asked her to take him to the area where his family had lived. His mother met him but she did not recognise him because he was so thin. When he told her that he was her son, she cried uncontrollably and he put his arms round her thin body and reassured her gently between his own sobs of relief. 'I can't believe you are alive,' she said. 'You were the one I spoilt. I thought he will never survive these terrible times.'

'Where are my brothers and sisters?' he asked. They were a family of nine, four brothers and five sisters: only his youngest sister was left, his three brothers and four sisters had all been killed by the Khmer Rouge.

His mother told him, 'Your father died of starvation; he was broken-hearted, calling for you and your dead brothers and sisters. He didn't know you were alive.'

Breaking down as he recalled this awful reality and brushing away the tears that ran down his face, he said,

'There are wounds brought about by Pol Pot and his men; wounds deep down in my mind and deep down in my heart that will never be healed.'

Barnabas served in the underground church until 1985 when there was a warrant out from the communist Vietnamese occupying forces to kill him. Throughout these tumultuous years he wrote songs of praise and produced Cambodian music and worship to broadcast throughout Cambodia through the Far East Broadcasting Company. There were many incidents of divine protection as he secretly gave the recorded cassettes to expatriate Christians who worked for non-governmental organisations (NGOs). Food was scarce and they were often hungry and frightened of repercussions from the soldiers of the Vietnamese occupation forces who hunted down anyone who was practising Christianity.

The search for Barnabas became so intense that he and his wife fled to Thailand to reach a refugee camp. At the end of January 1985 he made a decision to cross the sea to Thailand but he was arrested again, this time by Vietnamese marine guards. In September that year as they were over the Thai border, they were arrested by the Thai police. From the police station they were transferred to barbed wire cages and sent to three consecutive holding centres. Barnabas' wife and children eventually reached Site Two camp while he remained for a while in a police cell. He escaped one night and resumed the long hazardous walk in the direction of the refugee camp. It was a long, difficult journey and just when his strength was at a low ebb, he found a church in Drat that the Verners had planted and took refuge there until he was fit enough to continue his journey to Site Two camp in Thailand. Before the family were separated they frequently washed their clothes in rivers and at times when they had no food they were often surprised to find a large fish caught in their wet clothes.

In November 1985 after being separated from one another, Barnabas arrived at Site Two camp where the family stayed for eight years in conditions of hardship, deprivation and some deadly shelling. Barnabas continued to pastor a Cambodian church and co-pastor a Vietnamese church in the camp. Strengthened by Christ he never stopped writing and creating music for the body of Christ.

Site Two camp in Thailand had 170,000 Cambodians who were driven out of the country in the nine years following the Vietnamese overthrow of the Pol Pot regime in 1979. They were classified as displaced persons and had to stay there while western politicians argued over the problems and came to no definite decisions. Most of these refugees had left Phnom Penh and other towns because there was no food and no future in their homeland. Site Two camp was five square miles of primitive huts, open sewers; nothing grew there, not one palm tree, no vegetation: yet this was the only home for thousands of Cambodians who waited and waited with nothing to do and no hope of any future.

No nation in modern times had been through such trauma as the Killing Fields; but this was succeeded by the invasion of the Vietnamese communists who were nearly as bad in their brutal rule. The invasion brought about a political stalemate; there was no peace and the outside world forgot. Site Two had a makeshift hospital, amputees lay on dirty camp beds; flies, inadequate supplies of medicines, and heat from the shanty roofs were some of the problems facing health workers who tried to bring some hope in an atmosphere of hopelessness. This spilled over into the camp and many of the patients were refugees who had attempted suicide.

There was a primitive workshop for wooden legs that were fitted on the amputees, but in this camp there were

2,000 needing help to walk on these artificial limbs. While they waited for help there was nothing to do but sit and hope that one day they could start life again somewhere. United Nations Border Relief Operation lorries and tanks brought 500 tons of rice and half a million gallons of water every week. There was no tap water in the camp. To feed and water these people was costing £20 million a year, but the western world had no interest in their plight because the Soviet Union, China and Vietnam were all involved in supporting the puppet regime in Cambodia.

Barnabas with his wife and children tried to settle into life in this refugee camp. They lived in a little hut with a sack of second-hand clothes and handouts of rice and tinned fish; without this, they would have starved to death.

However Barnabas knew this hopelessness could be replaced with hope in spreading the gospel message to the rest of the refugees, so he set about finding a way to introduce them to the Saviour. He began Hope English School in the camp and through this avenue many came to know Christ. When there were many converts he led a Bible school in the camp and began systematic Bible teaching so they would have the necessary skills to plant churches when the day came for them to return to Cambodia. His vision for his own life and that of those around him was that they had hope and prayed for the time when God would allow them to return to their homeland to reignite the embers of the dying church and fan it into life.

In 1988 while still in Site Two camp, Barnabas was having his daily Bible reading and worship time with the Lord. He had a remarkable vision which he later described to me.

Barnabas' vision

It was in 1988 at ten o'clock in the evening, when my wife and all the children were woken up by a strange noise made by me talking to somebody at night. I received a vision from the Lord and I was talking to the Lord audibly so that my wife and all the children could hear me. In the vision I saw a pond filled with lotus flowers and I asked the Lord, 'What is it all about?' He explained to me that this was Cambodia dominated by Buddhism, because the lotus represents the life of Buddha, struggling in the mud of the sinful nature of man, striving to become an enlightened sage. Then the lotus came out of the water with fragrance and the reputation of the Buddha is that it is one of the great philosophies of the east. But in the back of that lotus pond I saw a green pasture with a line of trees, beautifully planted with evergreen leaves but no fruit. I asked the Lord again, 'In the vision Lord, what is it speaking about?' and the Lord told me that this is the beauty of Cambodia with no fruit, as Cambodia has accepted Buddhism as the state religion. The religion sounds good, the teaching sounds good, but the promises made by the people cannot be put into practice. There is no fruit in people's lives. People are still bound in the yoke of slavery and deception.

Then I saw a horse that was walking on the green pasture and destroying the beauty of the pasture and this is the experience of the Killing Fields that finally killed an estimated 1.8 to 3 million Cambodian people. It destroyed the infrastructure, the social structure, as well as brainwashing the Cambodian dignified mentality that made it a giving nation. It has now become a begging nation: people of good heart but now very selfish and self-orientated. And then I saw a cosmic blackout and in the sky there appeared a throne and on the green pasture before the throne, I saw hundreds of thousands, countless precious stones! I saw those pieces of gems dancing, moving backward, forwards, sideways, as if they were praising the Lord with the word 'Hallelujah!'

I looked up to the throne: it changed and I saw two heads of the Nagas: they are cobra heads, some with five heads and some with seven heads. You can find these heads of the Nagas on the National Independence Monument. They are recognised by the constitution of Cambodia as the founders of the nation. There are a lot of stories told about the Buddhist enlightenment that relate to the coiling Naga. You can find some Buddhist statues sitting on the coiling Naga or snake to protect him from the rain: also there is the Water Festival commemorated yearly especially when the Tonle Sap returns in November [the Tonle Sap is a huge freshwater lake in north Cambodia; it is also a river which flows from the lake into the capital city Phnom Penh. There is a confluence of four rivers near the royal palace – the Upper Mekong, the Lower Mekong, the Bassac and the Tonle Sap rivers. The Tonle Sap reverses the course of its waters at a fixed time. In the dry season, the waters go south east. In the rainy season, they go up towards the north east], to pay homage to another king of Naga. His name is the Marble Fang. It is believed that this king of Naga, the Marble Fang, when he is happy, will prosper Cambodia with rain to give enough water; but if he is not happy, drought will follow, so he is the god of prosperity for Cambodia. This is why in Cambodia there are many Naga statues in the Buddhist temples: even in the National Independence Monument and at any bridge or water reservoir. You will find the Nagas everywhere.

Then I saw in the vision the throne with two Nagas' heads, one on the right side and the other one on the left side. I said to the Lord, 'Lord this is not your throne because the devil is at work in the church' and the Lord explained to me, that false teaching, cultic teachings are coming to Cambodia. The church in Cambodia will be deceived by false prophets and so in 1992 a strong cultic group came from Canada, New Apostolic Church, and they approached some members of the parliament and they were converted and accepted by the communist government to operate in Cambodia. Now they claim to have 35 church buildings all over Cambodia but most of them are now empty buildings. They believe that the Apostle of Cambodia can pray for the salvation of the dead and this really fits with the Cambodian mentality that cares for their deceased parents and loved ones.

And then the Lord showed me the second throne and I saw two tails; one on the left of the throne in heaven so I asked the Lord, 'Why are there two tails of the Naga and what is it all about?' The Lord said the church in Cambodia will experience division and church splits: this is the work of the devil and then by 1993 denominationalism and specially the patronage as well as the poverty mentality came into the Cambodian church. It is a nation that is just recovering from communism, so the reality of poverty was acute but it is worse when some leaders of the church still have the poverty mentality. It was easier [sic] for the Lord to get the people of Israel out of Egypt but to remove the picture of it out of their minds was very difficult. The same thing has happened to the church leadership in Cambodia. Many of the leaders today, instead of asking the Lord for the divine strategy to develop church growth, they learn to depend totally on external resources. It is good to have them in the early stage of church growth but external resources cannot guarantee the church growth. When we were children we needed help to grow but when we are grown up we need to work ourselves.

The second state of church growth in Cambodia is the church with divisions and church splits by denominational leaders. Each one has his own little kingdom concept, so they lose the body of Christ and the kingdom concept, becoming more denomination centred. Then I saw the third throne with full splendour and glory, with no heads of the Naga and no tails of the Nagas. I said to the Lord, 'This is your throne!' I saw the precious jewels and those gem stones all dancing before the Lord. I joined with those jewels and I became as one of the jewels in the sight of the Lord.

Barnabas left Site Two camp in 1993, Cambodians who were in Thailand having been told to go back for the elections organised following the Paris Peace Accord. It was a day he had dreamed of for years while he waited in the refugee camp. But those years were not wasted as he had trained 53 church leaders in the School of Workers in the camp. They also returned to spread the gospel message throughout the provinces.

That day arrived when, travelling by train and bus, he was at last in the capital city with his wife, three daughters and three grandsons: but he had no money and no home. His daughter Shalom had been four when they arrived at Site Two camp and she was now twelve years old. He said to his children, 'Now we are back in our homeland, we can walk about freely.' His daughter replied, 'What is the difference? This doesn't look much better, but there are palm trees.' There were no trees in the camp. Barnabas felt elated at being free but concerned for the future and how he could begin life again with no resources. Everything in the camp had been free; food, clothing, basic medical care and at least a roof over their heads: primitive though it had been.

Barnabas remembers with great gratitude the kindness shown by someone from England and Sophal Ung from America, who arranged for him to be accommodated in rooms at their church. Attending a service there for the first time he felt deeply emotional as he heard them sing some of the songs he had composed in the dark days, on the run from the communist police. They were indeed 'songs in the night' as he composed them lying on his stomach in intense pain from a severe bout of rheumatoid arthritis and painful bleeding haemorrhoids. Barnabas was delighted to see evidence of many more churches worshipping the Lord than he had ever seen. But he had a burning desire to be a blessing to the body of Christ and God's instrument to continue rebuilding the Khmer church in a way that was in keeping with Cambodian culture.

For the first three months he helped with the church work and during that period met the Verners and other members of the SAO team. He spent hours in prayer asking the Lord to direct him into the pathway chosen for him. Looking for a small house to rent he discovered that the rents had risen astronomically. The smallest apartment cost between three and five hundred dollars per month. His wife encouraged him to take a step in faith, find a home and trust the Lord for the finance. They found a home and they were blessed with a gift which covered the first two months' rent.

Barnabas felt the 53 School of Workers 'graduates' from Site Two were essential for the rebuilding of a strong church that would survive the attacks predicted in the vision he had had five years previously. These men were trained and schooled in hardship and trials and were used of God to plant strong churches. The strategies they were taught are of significance to the west where the church is declining with affluence, compromise and weak commitment. Our views on mission need to be updated as we consider these concepts.

The Cambodians who knew the Lord, needed help from the west to rebuild the 'broken walls' that existed in Cambodia [See chapter twenty-one reference to Nehemiah]. Previously missionaries had been used by God in four areas, pioneering, parenting, preparing and partnering, but today Cambodians can do the first two phases well. They are using their heart language and know what is appropriate for the culture. They can plant new churches more effectively than expatriates; and they can disciple and mentor others because they understand how much pain they have suffered in the past. When they speak about faith, they have had to practice it in hard times so they know what their experience has taught them. The urgent need is for preparing and partnering Cambodians because early missionaries often did not teach skills on church management or leadership. Even today some expatriates teach repentance and witnessing but nothing further. The Cambodian church was greatly blessed in the past by Chhirc Taing's godly leadership, spiritual gifts and ability in church management. These essential components for healthy church growth are still needed today.

As Barnabas sought to help the fledgling church grow to maturity he taught seven core values.

1. Meaningful fellowship. Having been rejected by family relatives, many of the new converts needed to make new relationships in a loving environment where they were loved and nurtured. All the basic teachings of the Bible had to be solid, sure and sweet, rather than high-sounding theology.
2. Intimate worship is an essential ingredient for a fruitful life so new converts should be able to participate in the worship time. They must learn to know God personally in a deep way as a friend but also have a sense of his majesty and greatness.

3. Powerful prayer is an essential priority. Why are prayer meetings so poorly attended in the west? Without powerful intercessory prayer there will be no church growth.
4. Cheerful giving is a principle that has to be established even where there is poverty. Some places in a developing country do need partnership with western missionaries to help them to learn ways of earning a living so they can in turn give. This is where the necessity of holistic ministries plays such an important part.
5. In a growing church everyone should be encouraged to have a part practically, since we are called into a royal priesthood.
6. Everyone must learn to serve and have a servant attitude towards one another, each valuing others above themselves.
7. Effective evangelism is an essential part of the local church's work. There is a need for new converts to know the Saviour of the world not just a Saviour from America or the 'white man's religion'.

If these seven core values are established the church will grow and mature in the faith.

Barnabas sums up the challenge for quality leadership using the acronym SHAPE.
- Leaders must have *Spiritual gifts* in communication, teaching and singing.
- A *Heart for God* and for his people is essential; in a church people need to feel loved and cared for.
- They must possess *Ability to teach*, and know how to govern a church with godly principles of discipline maintaining biblical truths in this area.

- *Personality* is important but with this they must be able to work as a team. Differences in personality can lead to church splits. Watch out for the lone ranger, who will not confide in the elders and has to be in control of everything. It is essential to have leaders who can work together with others.
- The last essential is *Experience*. They must have experience with God personally both in knowing forgiveness and being able to forgive.

Some of these attributes may be missing in a leader, for example he may have spiritual gifts but he can't work in a team. Godly leaders learn to play soccer (as a team) but they must never learn boxing.

Quality resources are badly needed to rebuild a strong church in Cambodia. Barnabas commented:

> In the west you have Bible dictionaries, study aids: all sorts of commentaries, inspiring biographies: remember we have very little. How can we preach with quality and accuracy if we have no books with sound teaching? We need sustainability in the grace of giving with help in [the] income generation. Cambodia has a poverty mentality so we do need to have a prosperity mentality to erase the dependency. Everyone supports their children until they can earn a living; similarly we need support until we can earn a living. My vision for Cambodia is that we can be a giving and a sending church in the future to bless the body of Christ throughout the world.

Barnabas went on to explain that Cambodia's first coalition government had two prime ministers (two heads). This could not and did not last.

As we look at the life of the church in Cambodia we see the same thing happening, many associate pastors are not happy to remain as associate pastors: after the church reaches a certain number, for example fifty members regularly attending, then the church will split in two. Nationally we are trying to work together in unity with Paul, known as Paul of Cambodia, Revd Pon Sokha [not his real name], the president of the Evangelical Fellowship of Cambodia (EFC) today, and Revd Heng Cheng who is the General Secretary. Differences between leaders arise, which we try to bridge. Sometimes we succeed and on a few occasions rifts continue, but this body, the EFC was founded to bring about unity and we have experienced many blessings as we learn to work together.

CHAPTER FIVE:

Turbulent Times:
A return to democracy

The road to democracy from a communist state has proved to be a stormy time full of uncertainties. The Khmer Rouge continued to fight against the government from their bases along the Thai border. In September 1993 Prince Sihanouk was recrowned king and his wife Monique became queen. The country's full name is The Kingdom of Cambodia. During this difficult period the church was growing and by 1994 estimates suggested a membership of about five thousand. There was an attempted right-wing coup and Phnom Penh was a dangerous place at night. King Sihanouk undoubtedly brought a semblance of stability as king but his health was declining and he was diagnosed with cancer. He made frequent visits to Peking for treatment.

SAO Cambodia encouraged Marie Hill to help some of the returning refugees obtain employment. There were still many young people who had no place they could call home. Marie is an artist and a jeweller and had worked in a Thailand refugee camp where she had taught the refugees art and crafts. On one visit I enjoyed a day at the Rajana (Craft) Centre. There was a workshop on the ground floor where silk-weaving looms were made. When I arrived I was surprised at the number of young people who were happily

Marie and Joseph Hill

at work producing a variety of beautiful handicrafts. Young men were making silver jewellery and others were painting pictures on silk. There was a variety of greetings cards and girls were busy at the silk looms making some beautiful quality Cambodian silk. I decided to buy a length of this silk knowing how pleased Thida would be to see once again the fabrics she had worked on before all the tragedies hit her family. Many of the young people slept on the floor of the craft shop as they had nowhere to go. In the evenings Marie led Bible studies with them and almost every young person who has worked with Marie has become a Christian and is part of a Khmer church.

Marie told me: 'In the camp the Cambodian children loved drawing and they would sit happily at work, long after the others had wandered off for something else to do.' She showed me some remarkable pencil drawings, and told me about an artist, Borey, a returning refugee. He had been totally unable to draw after some traumatic experiences during the Pol Pot years. He listened attentively to the gospel message, and was a regular attender at their evening Bible studies. Receiving love, compassion and spiritual help through Marie, Borey renewed his career as an artist.

Cambodian society is noted for its artistic talent, drama, music and arts. Though the country had been at war for more than 25 years, and despite the reign of terror with Pol Pot, where even music was forbidden, creativity survived. Even walking round abject, poor squatter areas you can still find 'beauty in ashes'. Rajana (Cambodian Crafts) began training destitute returnees, amputees, widows, and partially sighted people, in skills that enabled them to earn enough to feed themselves and their families. Marie was fluent in the Khmer language and with the contacts she had made in the refugee camp she planted a church in Kirivong which has flourished to this day. Each participant was treated equally and without prejudice, regardless of creed or background. Those who made a commitment to Christ were encouraged to attend one of the indigenous churches where they were cared for in a culturally appropriate way.

From this brief sketch we see how the Cambodian church that refused to die, was revived and started to grow. It was, however, not without serious problems of divisions, disunity, and strife that sadly were caused by inappropriate missions offering money and resources to help it become a western-style church. There were moral crises; AIDS became a serious threat, and the needs again were overwhelming.

Jim and Agnes Verner were both working long hours to strengthen the national church, and alongside this big commitment, Agnes had established the Khmer School of Language, facilitating all the SAO team to be fluent in Khmer, but also helping other NGOs, diplomats and a wide variety of people to learn both English and Khmer. Through this there were people in government departments who were led to Christ. The school now has another branch in Sihanoukville, a school of sewing to help the poor and a Mercy Home for orphans.

But the church was growing rapidly and many of the Khmer who had sought freedom from oppression found Christ. Seekers were converted through Christian relatives and friends who had witnessed fearlessly, while others had believed from evangelism in the camps. Boldness replaced fear in witnessing and suspicion and hatred gave way to holiness of life and separation from social sins.

A Christian movement rooted in Khmer culture swept the country under the leadership of mature national pastors. Remarkable results emerged in people's lives and believers throbbed with the pride of being rooted deeply in Khmer Christian culture. Pastors Barnabas and Paul with their co-workers were part of this movement and they were unique because of their history of suffering and unprecedented poverty under Pol Pot.

Some saw only the downside to this country because alongside these developments ran divisions in the new church: pockets of violence still erupted from time to time with guns being easily bought in the markets, and it was common knowledge that there was a booming trade in child trafficking with so many unwanted children in the streets. HIV and AIDS were increasing at alarming rates and there were slum areas that shocked the onlooker. A balanced view was needed and it could be found in the good news.

One of the abandoned orphans was adopted by Marie. Nigel and Milet Goddard had their first son, and Mary, who had played such an important part in the children's work at the Development Centre, married Peter Barnett, SAO's administrator based in Phnom Penh. Jim Verner's experience in Thailand had taught him that there are always tensions and problems to overcome and his spiritual input was of immense value to the team. Cambodia had been robbed of its identity and culture and moral standards were abysmally low, so much so that, as it struggled to grow, the church showed a tendency for its light to dim.

This was not surprising and not any different from the Corinthian church that Paul wrote to in 1 Corinthians 1:4-6 at the beginning of the church era whose dissolute lifestyle permeated that church. 'I always thank God for you because of his grace given you in Christ Jesus. For in him you have been enriched in every way – in your speaking and in all your knowledge – because our testimony about Christ was confirmed in you. Therefore you do not lack any spiritual gifts as you eagerly wait for our Lord Jesus Christ to be revealed. He will keep you strong to the end, so that you will be found blameless on that day of our Lord Jesus Christ.' The apostle Paul strongly affirmed the church and that was an encouraging sign of the Lord's patience with his people. Similarly, we can expect God to move across this land of Cambodia in revival blessing despite the moral and spiritual debauchery that can be seen all around.

There are rural church planting ministries and also programmes to target university students, so that among the educated there may be government leaders who can testify to Christ. Nor have the nation's weak and downtrodden been neglected. Full-time staff members of another Christian NGO reach the poorest of Cambodia's children who live amid the filth of squatter-slums. Their Hope ministry is in the process of establishing 40 weekly programmes directed towards 3,000 underprivileged children. To facilitate this, 8 Cambodian staff and 20 assistants replicate the ministry of local churches, thus enabling children and their parents to receive further teaching and pastoral care. Apart from this, however, a strong indigenous movement has spread across the land, spearheaded by Cambodian pastors who emphasise the need to apply Christ's redemptive work in culturally relevant forms.

Jim Verner was involved in the setting up of the Evangelical Fellowship of Cambodia (EFC) advising board members to have nationals in the leadership and not westerners. Paul was chairman for six years and Barnabas was vice-chairman. When Paul stepped down, Revd Pon Sokha took the presidency and Revd Heng Cheng became the general secretary. As a member of the EFC, Jim challenged expatriate workers not to hinder the Khmer church by apparent affluence, offering dollars instead of Christ. He advised those seeking to plant churches to recognise the gifts of the national Christians and be careful to build churches that had a cultural relevance.

By 1998 some became exhausted with the seemingly endless problems. Their commitment to serve this volatile country was put to the test in a number of ways. Unfortunately there are well-intentioned Christians who go to serve the Lord in Cambodia but they are not prepared for the essential training in spiritual warfare that is so necessary if they are to become of use to rebuild the church. Many fell by the wayside while others tried to build a western style church that did not take into consideration the cultural needs of the Khmer people. Jim and Agnes had a vital ministry in this area and they were frequently called upon to help with moral problems and counselling Christians who were totally unable to cope with the pressures.

The fledgling church was growing but there were also tensions due to the precarious security situation as demonstrated in the following extract from the *Phnom Penh Post*:

A Japanese tourist was robbed of money, passport and air ticket by two men with a rifle at the ready. A man shot and killed himself after killing his pregnant wife and four others of his family. He always pointed a gun at his wife when he was drunk. A cyclo driver was killed by a grenade after an argument with four pedestrians. A palm wine dealer was seriously injured when he fell from a tree after being attacked by ants. Two robbers were shot and killed by district police when they tried to flee a robbery. A soldier fired his AK47 three times during a quarrel with his brother. The bullets seriously injured a neighbour. A grenade thrown by an unidentified person killed a police officer and wounded his neighbour. Two robbers and a policeman were killed in a gun battle; three others were wounded in the fighting which included the use of three smoke grenades. An elderly man from Prey Veng Province died when struck by a train. The victim had come to Phnom Penh to meet his son from Canada. The accident took place as he walked on the track near Phnom Penh University.

The Killing Fields era was over but what a backlash remained! We need to be aware of the political situation in Cambodia today in order to have a better understanding of its problems. There was a serious threat to the land with foreign companies logging in the rain forest areas, and selling off land belonging to local minorities for quick money-making crops. There are often reports of corruption among officials and ministers and this undermines trust and confidence in government. In addition there is the never ending problem of millions of landmines that still needed clearing.

When I visited Cambodia in 1995 I flew to Battambang with Claire Davies who had pioneered the optometry work for SAO Cambodia. She had set up an optometry shop and trained an amputee in optometry skills. I observed a Bible on the girl's work bench and Claire told me she regularly attended the local church. I was delighted to see several churches in Battambang but at the same time shocked at the number of amputees that sat on the roadside begging. Claire arranged for me to visit a landmine victims' hospital, and it was well run, but the sight of so many young men with no legs and some with an arm missing as well was depressing. There were also little children who had lost limbs.

Claire and I went into a country area where together with Help Age she held sight testing clinics. There was evidence of the political unrest as seen in the number of army vehicles with armed forces on the poorly kept roads. But quite a large number of the soldiers came to the mobile clinic to have their sight tested.

In 1997 the two main parties of the uneasy coalition agreed to hold elections in November 1998. Both parties had been experiencing political violence – offices razed to the ground, signs torn down and political assassinations. Tensions ran high between the coalition parties. At least 11 people were killed and 119 wounded in a grenade attack in an anti-government protest in March. The United Nations were invited again to monitor the elections as they had done five years earlier.

Despite the outward turmoil and dangerous conditions everywhere, by 1998 the church was growing faster than at any time in its history. There was liberty to hold meetings and to propagate the gospel. There were Christians in every province, and it was estimated that there were 80,000 Christians in the country. The combined ministries of the SAO team made a significant contribution but there were many other people and missions who made a great impact with nationals leading the churches.

CHAPTER SIX:

The Brooding Storm: Political Unrest

In 1998 Cambodia made world headlines as reports of Pol Pot's death circulated. He was found in the last guerrilla jungle hideout close to Anlong Veng and was unrepentant to the last. He had a fitting funeral pyre of old tyres and refuse. It was a difficult year with trials and severe setbacks for the SAO team but it began with a great deal to thank God for and the growth of the church was amazing. In 1990 Phnom Penh had ten house groups; in 1998 it had 50; various reasons being cited for such encouraging growth. The Khmer had sought jobs, free medical treatment, and freedom from oppression: they found all these and Christ as well through holistic programmes.

The work of Pastor Barnabas achieved remarkable results as he sought help from suitable organisations such as World Vision. They began a programme of community health in Oudong District, Kandal. World Vision's low-key involvement enabled pastors Barnabas and Paul to sensitively minister among the receptive villagers, where as yet no Christians existed. Its remit was to minister to the whole person as taught in Micah 5:4,5: 'He will stand and shepherd his flock in the strength of the LORD, in the majesty of the name of the LORD his God. And they will live securely, for then his greatness will reach to the ends of the earth. And he will be their peace.'

Paul of Cambodia was working with Barnabas at this time and Paul's gift in Bible teaching was shown in powerful and clear expositions of Scripture interspersed with a clear form of dialogue, which communicated readily with those wanting to accept Christ. Barnabas ministered among villagers at all levels using local analogies to reinforce his message. This powerful ministry also covered 36 slum areas in Phnom Penh complemented by Christian NGO health workers. It was quickly followed up by Bible study groups under Khmer leadership. That all of these ministries complemented each other in tandem, pays tribute to the spiritual rapport between expatriates and Khmer pastors.

The Oudong pattern has been followed in SAO's ministry as well, particularly at the Aquaculture Development Centre in Tual Krasang District, where the children's outreach and the gospel message has established a new church with locally trained leadership. Khmer leadership is rapidly becoming the spearhead of spiritual advance on a countrywide basis today. These teachers know God; they understand their own people and they have strong convictions regarding their task. At this crucial time in Cambodia's history there was a clarion call to prayer as the General Elections were to take place in July 1998 and changes would take place in government that would affect everyone.

Nigel and Milet Goddard's work had been richly blessed by the Lord and the fish farming projects were now helping 337 households, and there were farmer clubs in 20 locations. By this method one village that had learnt the skills was able to pass them on to the next village. Nigel and Milet both saw the need for eventually handing over the project into Khmer hands for long-term sustainability. 'We must live out the reality of our relationship as sons and daughters of the living God. The church is the community of the body of Christ, a visible evidence of his presence. We are God's chosen people to demonstrate the kingdom in this world. There is a constant temptation for us to resist and conform to the brokenness of the surrounding society. Our lives must be such that we individually, and even more so communally, are a convincing picture of Christ's dawning kingdom. The challenge to each one of us, whether in Cambodia or elsewhere is to be leading lives hallmarked with love, lives that are salt and light, pointing people to their Creator and the wholeness that all mankind so deeply needs.'

Every avenue of input by SAO had been blessed by the Lord, but as is so often the case, blessing can be followed by a time of trial. One attack followed another, and some were caught off guard. Mary, the Khmer lady mentioned earlier who was such a blessing in the children's work, attended a Khmer church where there was a relatively new convert in need of employment. There was a vacancy at the SAO office for a night guard, so the new convert applied for it and was eminently suitable for the position. He was married and his wife was expecting their first baby; everyone felt it was right for him to have the job. All the premises were guarded for protection, as armed robberies were common.

The July 1998 elections passed off relatively peacefully but no party won enough seats to form a government. Hun Sen's Cambodian People's Party won 62 of the 122 seats but this was not enough to secure the necessary two-thirds of the seats. The (FUNCIPEC) Royalist Party won 43 seats and the rest went to the Sam Rainsey Party, so a coalition needed to be formed. But talks between the parties failed with allegations of electoral fraud and intimidation threats. Opposition supporters arranged mass demonstrations and marches, which were peaceful until grenades were thrown into Hun Sen's house, resulting in a police crackdown. There were claims of beatings, tortures and murders, including that of Buddhist monks; it was a critical time in the history of Cambodia. The country could not continue politically or economically with the stalemate. Poor harvests

Contryside mode of transport

made prices reach an all-time high: the World Food Programme reported that Cambodia's economy was suffering from a decline in foreign aid, investment and tourism. The United Nations Development Programme said the country's administration was virtually paralysed. It was a complex situation that needed urgent prayer and a miracle to bring the parties together. Phnom Penh had an uneasy peace; there were gunshot sounds at night and reports of escalating violence. Some embassies including that of the Philippines were advising their people to evacuate and Milet Goddard had to return to her brother's home in the Philippines with their children. They reluctantly said goodbye to Nigel.

The team was on the 'alert' and had been briefed by Nigel Goddard, who was team leader at the time, to take extra care in all their activities. It was monsoon season and violent storms seemed to brood over the city with threatening darkness. Lightning and thunder lit up the black skies and rain poured down in torrents. Even the hungry dogs sought refuge under the tin roof of a slum dwelling. Suddenly fierce winds blew up throwing down dead palm fronds into the piles of refuse that accumulated in the pot-holed roads. The Verners had gone home early from their visit to a village as they were aware of the political unrest. They spent a long time praying but frequently they could not hear one another with the loud claps of thunder. The lightning lit up their darkened room and made it impossible to sleep. At midnight the storm abated and they fell into a light slumber, only to be woken by a loud knock on the door at dawn just a few hours later. It was the day guard with an ashen face: 'I've tried phoning the night guard at the SAO office but there's no reply. Can you come and see if he is all right?'

Immediately Jim dressed, ran downstairs and across the road to the office. The main door was wide open. Cautiously he turned the handle of the office door and froze when he saw the blood-splattered walls and overturned furniture. Lying on the floor was the body of the night guard who had been brutally attacked; there were pools of blood. Reaching for the phone lying on the floor, Jim dialled for Nigel. His heart was pounding as he ran back and called Agnes. 'Hurry, something terrible has happened!' Nigel arrived quickly and called the emergency services but it was too late. The guard was dead.

Tears ran down everyone's faces as they thought of this man's earnest commitment to Christ. What terrible news for his widow who was expecting their first baby! When the police arrived they looked round the office and asked if anything had been stolen. Jim had already noticed that the safe was missing and he knew that SAO had drawn an additional sum of money out of the bank the day before to be ready for a possible evacuation of the team if the political situation worsened. But this was only known to a few people. The safe also contained passports and other essential documents. As the police took control, everyone had to account for their whereabouts and the search for the culprit began. It seemed that the thieves had had information about the money. Perhaps there was an inside informer? An awful suggestion, and yet a possibility. The police began their inquiries, commencing with each member of the staff. Shock waves hit everyone, and the episode was reported in the newspapers

It was a very black day in the history of SAO in Cambodia. Everyone felt numb that this new convert had died such a violent death, as he had clearly tried to defend himself and prevent the robbery. The door had been forced open and there was clear evidence of a struggle. The violent storm that had echoed across the city until midnight, returned in the morning; heavy black clouds emptied torrents of monsoon rain and the fierce lightning and claps of thunder rolled overhead, adding to the gloom that enveloped everyone. The only consolation was that the guard had gone to his eternal home having embraced Christianity; but his widow would face having the baby with no husband to support her.

The tragedy had far-reaching effects, as no one wanted to remain in the building. The police were hunting the killer or killers as they suspected more than one was involved in the murder. It was a terrible time for everyone, especially the Verners, who had seen one murder in Thailand when the elder of one of their churches had been shot instead of Jim. They never dreamt they would face another murder – despite the violent society that still remained in Cambodia. SAO launched an appeal in England for funds to support the widow.

A decision was made to move the fish farming administration office to the Aquaculture Development Centre in Tual Krasang District which meant that it could no longer be used jointly as a church. This was a positive move so a small church was built and put under the leadership of a Khmer pastor. The church immediately grew despite the setbacks and many of the children that Mary had taught in the Sunday school asked their parents to come to the church; other relatives saw the love of Jesus in the team members who had cared for their physical needs first and afterwards invited them to hear about the Saviour's love. The church has continued to grow and is now a thriving Christian community in the place that was once an area of horrible atrocities by the Khmer Rouge. The message of the cross of Christ has triumphed over tragedy and jewels are being formed for the eternal city where the Prince of Peace will rule in all his beauty.

There were other events that shook the team: one member, who had been so helped by the Lord, defected in a distressing manner and returned to England. Such tragedies make you think deeply over these complex issues. Can you forfeit eternal life if you leave the pathway of faith? God has grace unlimited, and his heart is always to save to the uttermost. His compassion knows no end and yet he is a faithful God who waits for the wanderer to return home. How long can we wander away and how far can we go to forfeit our salvation? Over against the Father's love that is always looking for the prodigal to return home, there are some very serious scriptures that need to be considered. Hebrews 6:4: 'It is impossible for those who have once been enlightened, who have tasted the heavenly gift, who have shared in the Holy Spirit, who have tasted the goodness and the word of God and the powers of the coming age, if they fall away, to be brought back to repentance, because to their loss they are crucifying the Son of God all over again and subjecting him to public disgrace.'

Hebrews 3:12 has a timely warning for everyone, 'See to it, brothers, that none of you has a sinful unbelieving heart that turns away from the living God. But encourage one another daily, as long as it is called Today, so that none of you may be hardened by sin's deceitfulness. We have come to share in Christ if we hold firmly till the end the confidence we had at first.'

The weather remained stormy, dark clouds came over the usual sunny skies and emptied torrents of rain; perhaps the elements were trying to wash away these dreadful events. The atmosphere in the city was stormy politically, opposition supporters were still demonstrating and further violent skirmishes occurred on the streets. Political leaders met King Sihanouk to try to sort something out. The King appealed to his son, Prince Rannaridh, and Sam Rainsey to accept the election results. The new parliament was set to convene on 24 September to avoid a constitutional crisis. The occasion was historic with Hun Sen meeting his bitter rivals for the first time since Prince Rannaridh was ousted from power in July 1997. The National Assembly convened at Siem Reap as agreed, despite a rocket-propelled grenade being thrown at the procession as it made its way to the King's palace, killing one, and wounding others. Still no coalition was formed. Everyone prayed for stability but a miracle was needed to solve the divisions.

Thankfully God heard those prayers and in November a surprise agreement was reached, brokered by King Sihanouk after his son, Prince Rannaridh and premier Hun Sen finalised a complex deal. Everyone praised God that Hun Sen and Rannaridh put aside personal bitterness to form this coalition. Hun Sen is now sole prime minister, the post previously shared by both men, causing bitter rows over power sharing.

It is interesting to ponder these events in the light of the vision of Barnabas. Dualism was now past history politically but had it been erased in the church? Sadly there was evidence that dualism was not just one problem: divisions, disunity and splits were everywhere. The church was growing in spite of these complex problems, but when we study the epistles and the difficulties in the early churches, they too had their problems and divisions. Perhaps it will only be when Christ returns to take the church to be his heavenly bride that we shall then have that radiance that reflects the unity of the Godhead. While we are in these bodies that are so prone to sin we sadly only have a dim reflection of the future glory.

The western church with all its comforts and freedom to worship has its own share of disunity. Christians fight one another over small issues such as the colour of the carpet, or the praise songs that we sing. Godly pastors are sometimes the subject of unfair criticisms from ungrateful church members who don't always contribute positively. People lose sight of what the church is for: a place where we should all be worshipping God, reading his word and helping one another to grow. It is supposed to be a place of forgiveness, love and encouragement. In Ephesians 4:1 the apostle Paul writes from prison, 'I urge you to live a life worthy of the calling you have received. Be completely humble and gentle; be patient, bearing with one another in love. Make every effort to keep the unity of the Spirit through the bond of peace.'

The last of the Khmer Rouge leaders had surrendered, but it was a compromise when these leaders were actually greeted with handshakes, flowers and a lavish meal by Hun Sen. King Sihanouk, however, called the Khmer Rouge criminals and said there should be no pardons. The government needed balance between mercy on the one side and justice on the other. There is confusion in Cambodian minds because they hold an annual Day of Hate, dedicated to keep their anger alive at the Khmer Rouge, while these same men were being feted by Hun Sen. There were no perfect solutions to the political divisions; but the Lord of the Harvest was helping the Cambodian church to deal with its divisions and disagreements and at the same time was raising up leaders from the church to pray with the prime minister and King Sihanouk.

Despite all the setbacks God sees the needs of his people and he has wonderful plans for those who stay at 'the post' amid severe trials. These trials are always timed by God who sees the end from the beginning. It is all so easy to lose sight of an Almighty God who holds the universe in his hands and is in control, when our circumstances seem to fly out of our hands and we look at the future with fear and forebodings.

CHAPTER SEVEN:

Rivers of Blessing
at the Tonle Sap lake

After the evacuation Milet returned to Cambodia. Feeling relieved to be together again and making a fresh commitment to continue serving the Lord in this needy but volatile land, she and Nigel purchased a plot of land in a quieter part of the city to build a Khmer-style house. After all the dark events, their faith and calling had been sorely tried: but theirs was a faith that could stand the Refiner's fire. They were all the more committed to serving the Lord in this troubled nation. They reminded me of the verse in Psalm 92: 'The righteous will flourish like a palm tree, they will grow like a cedar of Lebanon; planted in the house of the Lord, they will flourish in the courts of our God.'

Nigel felt that SAO could be greatly strengthened by joining with other partners in Cambodia. After months of prayer and meetings with the Council, a decision was made to work in partnership with World Concern, the Summer Institute of Linguistics, Interact and Dan Mission. International Co-operation Cambodia (ICC) was the name of the new alliance and it was a very positive move forward. Nigel was the Executive Director of SAO at this point in the history of the mission so his new role in the conglomerate was to be part of the management team. He took on responsibility for human resource management as

A fish pond is flourishing in a village

the member with the longest service in Cambodia and the greatest fluency in the Khmer language. SAO ceased to have a separate registration with government in Cambodia where it now operates as part of ICC.

After this successful negotiating and strengthening SAO, Nigel moved on to a local non-governmental organisation where he is training Khmer development workers from various organisations including FAITH project, World Vision and Church World Service. Through all the difficulties Nigel maintained a steady trust in the Lord who gives us both good times and adversity to test our faith and help us to grow.

It is interesting to reflect on some unique characteristics of tropical palms. The life of the tree comes through its centre or heart, the sap going into the heart from the roots. In other trees the sap is in the exterior bark that protects the tree; removing the bark in a circle round the trunk can kill the tree. With the palm, no outward attacks can kill it but if dirt is allowed to remain on the palm and the dead fronds are not removed this can kill the tree. In the forest areas of Cambodia, you can see palm trees that have other small trees growing in them. This happens when bird droppings lodge in the untrimmed fronds, leaving small seeds, which grow in the rainy season. As the new tree uses nutrients from the palm, it gradually kills the tree. What a lesson there is for us in the palm tree. Let us keep our lives daily cleansed from sin, confessing it to the Lord for forgiveness. Palm tree Christians never change with circumstances: they are the same vibrant witnesses day after day because the life of Christ is in the centre of their beings.

The same principle of steadfast faith was seen in the Verners and their needs were supplied in an unusual way at this point of their service in Cambodia. They were asked to care for a house situated near the great Tonle Sap lake for six months. Committing this matter to the Lord in prayer and after seeking advice everyone felt it was specially ordered of the Lord, so they packed some of their belongings into their Land Rover and began the long difficult journey to the lake. I visited this lake with Agnes on my third visit to Cambodia and we enjoyed an evening in a rickety wooden boat that took us over the lake in a spectacular sunset. I was fascinated by life on the lake and had never seen people living in a floating village before.

After the Verners settled into their temporary home they celebrated Christmas with a distinct difference. Taking a boat taxi they joined the residents of the Tonle Sap lake. It was a hot sunny day with a brilliant blue sky and the view over the lake was stunning so they prepared themselves for evangelising in this beautiful area that Agnes and I had visited together two years previously. Appropriately Jim's vision for the work was taken from Ezekiel who saw a river flowing from the temple, the waters of which overflowed his ankles, knees, waist and head. This represents a man in earnest for his God; he is fully immersed in his job and dares to go head deep into God's work.

Spiritually, this is what residents of the lake required of evangelists who would impact them for Christ. SAO had already had some encouraging response from one floating village and was eager to keep up the momentum. The Verners enjoyed the thought of sharing the festive season with some of the residents on the lake. It would be impossible for us to imagine celebrating Christmas on the bare boards of a sampan boat belonging to a family of the floating village that nestled on the lake! Nevertheless the boat people's worship was simple, but the divine Presence profound.

The Verners had built bridges of friendship with some of the residents and found a great willingness to hear the gospel message. On Christmas Day they were welcomed on board the simple wooden sampan of Grandmother Patum. Christmas dinner was fish caught from the lake with some rice and seasonings, followed by mangoes and pineapple. In an atmosphere of deep reverence Grandmother Patum suddenly appeared from a small inner area and laid a new-born baby girl in Agnes' lap with the simple request: 'Please dedicate her to Jesus.' This was a special Christmas with a dedication for a lake baby and as they thought about the day, celebrating the birth of Jesus, the Saviour of the world, it reminded them of his invitation to the little children to come to him for a blessing all those years ago. Jim told them the story of the birth of Jesus in a simple stable in Bethlehem and how that baby was born to be the Saviour of the world. He was born to die on a cruel cross to pay the price for our sins. He still calls little children, and continues to live within these fragile frames which Scripture calls his temples.

This was a memorable event in the Verners' lives as they had never before taken a dedication ceremony on a boat!

Before them lay a tiny infant, born in poverty and housed on a humble sampan! That day she was dedicated to God replete with her innocent purity. Later she would hopefully accept Christ personally and live for him within this floating village culture. God's message to them that day was clear: 'Now watch me transform adults too. Then I shall sail the great lake in the lives of my boat people, manifesting myself in their villages through them.' They thanked the Lord for this baby and had a time of worship with the rest of the family. Not everyone could be accommodated on the sampan so their relatives moored a boat alongside and joined in the celebrations. As the day came to a close the evening shadows fell across the lake in colours of yellow and gold, silhouetting the boats and sending silver rays of sunshine over the floating village. God was doing a new work in establishing a floating church in this unusual setting of the floating village of the lake.

Christmas, however was not the Verners' first meeting with Grandma Patum and her extended family. Their initial contact happened unannounced four months previously when an expatriate nurse had invited them to look after her house very close to the lake, while she took further studies. Prior to the nurse's departure they invited her for discussions about the spiritual needs of the 'lake people'. That was when they reconnoitred the nearby floating village, praying that God would use them to bless the people there. That morning they dismounted the motorbike taxi and sought a boat taxi for an ostensible sightseeing tour of the village. They surveyed the score of waiting attendants and shot an arrow prayer heavenwards. 'Please Lord; lead us to the right person.'

From the mingling mass of possibilities they immediately located a middle-aged woman silhouetted specially for their benefit. They were more than delighted that she claimed to be a Christian, one of many without a church meeting in that floating village. This boat lady, Mrs Chee, adroitly navigated out from the jumble of boats that floated out of the narrow inlet of the lake beyond. They travelled along the spacious waterway, which was conveniently called Main Street; the police station on the right and a Shell station to the left running cheek-by-jowl with a floating pig-pen!

A travelling food and cigarette sampan plied its trade close to overhanging verandas where people could easily balance their bodies overboard to buy a desired product. Mechanics, boat builders, hairdressers and net weavers: they were all there, just as you might find in any roadside village. The locals waved a friendly welcome to them even though they felt like intruders into their unique lifestyle.

Understanding the Verners' errand, a delighted Mrs Chee escorted them to her boat home to meet her family. 'Not big enough for a church meeting,' she quietly observed. After prayer, Mrs Chee took them to a relative who had a larger facility. Main Street led into ragged avenues, winding every-which-way, depending on the rise and fall of the tide. They finally approached the destination in a small cul-de-sac overgrown with rotting waterweed and debris from the discarded refuse of the lake dwellers. In some areas of the lake the waters are too shallow to navigate at certain times of the year, depending on the movement of the Tonle Sap. In these shallow parts, water hyacinths grow vigorously and there are water lilies which I was told make a tasty soup!

A gracious hostess welcomed them and arranged a further meeting with selected friends who were nominal Christian families in Cambodia. Days later they returned, held discussions and suggested that their group request government permission to hold meetings legally. Later still, they met again rejoicing with their new friends that official recognition had been granted. At last they could meet but they didn't have a pastor. Fortunately the Verners were available temporarily to fill this slot that God had prepared. They estimated 50 families awaiting the word in their village alone. Four other nearby villages in the same district had nominal believers who also sought permission to hold Christian meetings; subsequently they would build their own Boat Church.

Agnes observed Mrs Patum's love in action for poor children of the community. She had already started a morning primary school in her boat, for people who could not afford private school on the lake. Up to 20 children have grasped this opportunity and attend the school where afternoons are open for religious instruction, and the Verners' participation was well received. Seeing the lack of any tools they took a small presentation of books, pencils and chalks, and other basic materials which touched the visionary teacher at a deep level. Someone asked, 'How about building a boat school which could double up as a church on Sundays?'

The Verners still had a large number of responsibilities in Phnom Penh and they had received a call from Ratanakiri, a province in the south east, to help with some problems in small new churches that were springing up in that remote area. For a while they commuted between the lake and Phnom Penh to assist this fascinating outreach. It is a harrowing trip between the village and Phnom Penh so they did this every four to eight days in order to fulfil obligations in the city. Their input to the village is of necessity limited now, but here is the good news; their vision to see God touching the lives in the floating villages of the lake is already being augmented even by grandmothers. Ezekiel's natural eyesight may have waned but his ever increasing vision of living waters flowing from

God's temple will yet inspire younger men to act. When I visited the lake in November 2003 I noticed a large boat with a cross on the roof clearly indicating that a church was in place.

The landlord of the house where the Verners were staying has subsequently followed up his interest in the faith. He frequently visited Phnom Penh attending church and signed up for a Bible correspondence course from the WEC headquarters.

CHAPTER EIGHT:

Return to Cambodia

The political background in the country seemed to be more promising with one prime minister, and the Khmer Rouge becoming a non-entity. Hun Sen hailed 1999 as the first peaceful year in decades, promising that the government would now focus on development. Cambodia had more international humanitarian aid agencies per capita than any other nation, but incredibly poverty still gripped 40 per cent of the population. Added to this, the environment had serious problems with the forests and fisheries being depleted at a dangerous rate.

Large areas of land had remained unused because of the landmine problem and efforts were being made to use this land far too quickly. Vast areas in the north west were still heavily mined and amputees continued to be a common sight. Skull and crossbone signs were everywhere warning people to stay out but in their desperate search for food these landmine warnings were being ignored. The *Phnom Penh Post* recorded:

> Two former guerrillas hiking from the Thai border were reported seeking for land on which to grow food. Hobbling along on one leg and crude wooden sticks they said, 'We can't wait for the de-miners. I'm terrified I will lose my one good leg but what can I do?' Experts estimate that 5 million mines still remain, and at the current clearance rate it will take until 2020 to clear the most fertile soil.

Added to this was another problem of frightening dimensions. AIDS was spreading at an alarming rate, with about 15 per cent of armed forces personnel believed to be infected with HIV, making them the second highest rate group after sex workers. It is a normal part of life in Cambodia for males to visit brothels and an estimated twenty-two people die each day from AIDS and half the victims are under twenty-five, with women being particularly vulnerable. There is a great need for more education and preventative health care to tackle this problem but there are dedicated Christians being led into work to address these needs. Presently Dr Doug Shaw is Public Health Physician HIV/AIDS and Health Advisor and he is working all hours to address these problems through his commitment to World Vision who see the desperate need to find some solutions to these complex issues.

Cambodia has become a trafficking place for women and children between surrounding countries who abuse and exploit them in brothels, factories, on construction sites and as beggars. More than 300,000 people have been caught up in such rackets, and the Cambodian government has joined with five other regional countries to stamp out this horror.

Nigel and Milet were excited at the prospect of tackling some of these issues through community health and development projects in some of the poorest villages. These practical ministries would bring the Light of the World and the knowledge of a God who would hear the cry of the needy and respond to their prayers. The FAITH project (Food And Income, Training and Health) began after discussions with EFC so they could link with existing health care ministries and work alongside local Christian groups.

The FAITH project extended to 40 villages, one of these being in the Svay Rieng Province, about 17 kilometres from the Vietnamese border. It already had a church, which had been started in 1985 by the fifty-three-year-old Khmer pastor. He is one of the few surviving pastors of the war years. The Lord had blessed this man's work with 150 members regularly attending the church but all were very poor, living on meagre diets with very little money to bring up their children. The pastor told Milet he was so happy to receive help to train the village people in technical skills such as fish farming and duck rearing. He said, 'I know we will not remain poor if we are willing to help each other and work hard.'

In 1999 there were several moves forward both in the political situation and in church growth and unity. Pol Pot was dead and Ta Mok, the Khmer Rouge military chief, was in prison awaiting trial. Delays in the trial had a variety of reasons; Hun Sen refused to have an international tribune, China was nervous about their former help to the Khmer Rouge coming out into the open, and western countries were apprehensive too, because there were British companies supplying landmines and at the same time having contracts to rebuild the roads. These were lucrative contracts when the landmines were constantly blowing up the roads.

By the end of the 1990s Christian missions were impacting the country significantly and new converts were being added to the church daily. One convert to Christianity hit headlines worldwide. Kaing Khek Iev, better known as 'Deuch', who was head of Toul Sleng Prison during the terrible years of 1975-79, has confessed to mass killings and also admitted killing eight westerners after they endured a month of torture. Deuch has made the most amazing revelation while languishing in prison and expecting to die. He told journalists that he had become a Christian.

Fully recognising his evil past, he said that he knew he had done very bad things in his life, and that it was OK for them to take his body because Jesus had his soul – it was time for him to bear the consequences of his actions, but he did not worry because it was up to Hun Sen and Jesus. The news report, in newspapers worldwide, did not say how Deuch heard the gospel but we will read of this later.

EFC was recognised by the government and it has a positive contribution in unifying the Christian churches. The torch that had been lit by Cambodian Christian Services was handed on to EFC. As the church grew so did the need for EFC to help with the building of co-operation and trust between the nationals and those coming to Cambodia to provide support and assistance in Jesus' name. Nigel and Milet were able to contribute to this process.

Most of the provinces now had some Christian input but alongside the positive work were serious problems of disunity in the province of Ratanakiri. As a member of EFC, and after discussions with Paul and Barnabas, the Verners were sent to Ratanakiri, where Jim worked with an expatriate to resolve differences with his Cambodian counterpart. It took time, but the success of that endeavour prompted a phone call two years later to ask if he would help set up a city-wide seminar, entitled, 'How to resolve conflict between expatriate NGOs and their counterparts.' It focused on expatriates only but representatives from between 50 to 60 organisations attended. Pastor Barnabas was invited along with Paul and Pastor Pon Sokha to form the discussion panel while Jim chaired the meeting. It was a very helpful and positive move forward; Jim spent hours working to assist unity in the rebuilding of the Cambodian church. The full impact of these negotiations had far-reaching effects particularly in Ratanakiri as we shall see later.

The national leaders of the EFC are remarkable chosen men with godly characters that have been formed through adversity. When I began writing this book I knew that I could not finish it without another visit to Cambodia to collate information and perhaps even have the privilege of meeting these men of faith who have been sovereignly used of God in the rebuilding of the Cambodian church. It was a major decision for me to return to Cambodia 2003 as my last visit in 1997 ended abruptly with illness. I had been advised by doctors not to return. After many weeks of prayer, seeking the Lord's direction through Bible reading, and listening for God's instructions, my husband felt clearly that it was right for me to return for this last visit. After medical check-ups even my doctor said it would be all right to go back.

As the plane from Bangkok touched down at Pochentong Airport, Phnom Penh, I felt deeply emotional to be back once more in this city I had grown to love so dearly. It was evening and the monsoon rains were falling heavily as the taxi drove through the darkened city. I noticed little street children washing their faces in the puddles; some barely three years old. I knew many, including WEC International, had gone to Cambodia to care for these children. I arrived at the hotel Milet had arranged for me and was amazed at the large luxury houses that were being built nearby, some next door to very poor wooden shacks. In the morning the sun was shining brightly and in God's amazing goodness, there was no more rain for the month I was in Cambodia. Everyone commented on how abruptly the monsoons had finished.

CHAPTER NINE:

Shepherds from the Camps

Barnabas invited me to his church on my first Sunday so we drove through the city early in the morning. I had been up at dawn as the city comes to life about five o'clock when the dawn chorus meets with cockerels crowing, dogs barking, street vendors calling their wares and the incessant honking of horns from the chaotic traffic. Bumping over pot-holed roads we finally arrived at a large house where there were many people arriving for the service. Climbing the two flights of stairs we entered the large auditorium where the band was already playing praise music.

Ten years had passed since I met Barnabas in the little apartment down an untidy street in Phnom Penh. He had returned from Site Two refugee camp and was starting a church in the front room of that home. Despite all the sufferings that he and his wife Boury had been through, they both had faces full of the joy of the Lord. On this occasion I was thrilled to see the large auditorium filled with so many singing praise songs to the accompaniment of a band. Pretty children in Khmer dress held tambourines and danced to the music.

The words of some hymns came on the screen with an English translation and it was a moving experience to join in songs that Barnabas had composed in the dark years of the Khmer Rouge. These songs touched the hearts of the singers so that the praise lifted us up to the heavenly realms. Instead of the small congregation of ten years ago there were about three to four hundred present and an atmosphere of thanksgiving to the God who had brought many through fiery trials to the present day. The memories of the service that day will forever be in my mind as one of the most outstanding experiences of the presence of God.

I wanted to meet the pastors who had gone out to the provinces when they returned to Phnom Penh from Site Two camp but time did not permit. Despite his heavy workload Barnabas came for a time of fellowship and told me what had happened to the Christians he had helped to nurture in the Site Two refugee camp.

He kept in touch with them and they are bearing fruit for Christ today. As they obtained jobs, or returned to the provinces where they were brought up, these messengers of the gospel have spread the faith in many areas throughout Cambodia. Smiling happily he said:

It is a privilege for me to live such a purpose-driven life to serve my Lord, my family and my people. As I travel around the country I meet many younger pastors who seem to know me so I ask them how they know me. They reply with such love, that they found Jesus in Site Two camp through seeing the practical demonstration of the love of Christ. This motivated them to become shepherds, to teach and train others to love the Saviour. God is so good, isn't he? He has allowed me to live to see a generation of pastors who are bearing fruit for Christ from those days of desolation in the camp. And now he is so good, for I am having the privilege of seeing the next generation responding to Christ's calling and my vision is to see every town and village know this wonderful message.

I thank God that he has placed me in a very strategic position as an encourager, a peace-maker, an equipper, a trainer, and a shepherd of the shepherds all under the leadership of the Lord Jesus Christ, the great Shepherd of the sheep.

Barnabas gave me examples of how these Christians were helping the church to grow.

Pastor Kong Kear

Pastor Kong Kear is married with six children and living in Banteary Mean Chey, a province close to the Thai border. They came back with no money and they decided to make cakes and sell them at the market place to earn a living and preach the gospel. He came to see me in Phnom Penh and told me he had been able to build a house of bamboo and thatch but it caught fire one day and was burnt to the ground. A missionary went to him and said, 'If you join my denomination we will build you a house.' He took this suggestion to God and he also asked me, 'Is this real brotherly love, he offers to build me a house, but it is conditional that I join his denomination?' He asked me if I had experienced this pain of being offered much needed help but making that conditional on me joining his church. I told him I had experienced this many times and I felt bitterness and anger at such conduct. After a while I had to take it to the Lord and he told me to forgive. When I forgave, the bitterness, pain and anger was removed. This man accepted the need to forgive so he went back and began to preach forgiveness and to teach the need to live together in harmony with one another.

Living in abject poverty, his preaching brought fruit and the church began to grow. He joined the church planters of the Bible Institute set up within this church building, and I was able to help him to live in a better situation. I stayed close to him and arranged for him to come to Phnom Penh each month to pray and have fellowship together. This man now pastors three churches; the mother church in his town Sisophon, and two others among the poorest people along the Thai border. The people he cares for are nomads, they move from place to place but he never gives up on them. Now he helps with another sister church that sprang up at the same time and is under the leadership of a man I looked after in the camp.

Pastor Moses

This man was sent to the hospital in the camp because he was seriously ill with meningitis. He was so ill that when he finally recovered, he had lost his memory and did not even know his name. While he was so ill in the camp he was transferred from one hospital to another and his wife left him in the lurch. Pastor Kong Kear's mother, compelled by the love of God, took care of him but he ended up in a psychiatric clinic with severe depression. His memory of all past events was erased including his name so when he partially recovered in the clinic he made a new name for himself: Moses. He is known as Pastor Moses today.

I lost track of him in the variety of hospitals in the camp because there were restrictions on our movements from one camp to another. One day a Jewish American called Dr Daniel came to find me and told me he had a patient called Moses who was asking for me. I told him I did not know anyone by the name of Moses. So Dr Daniel explained that it was a new name. He said Moses had told him that I was a man of my word and I had promised this man a coconut.

I asked the doctor to take me to this man after I had bought a young coconut. He took the coconut from me, drank the juice and then fell asleep for a long time. I was amazed that despite this severe memory loss Moses had a clear picture and remembered me.

Later I saw him enter my church in Site Two camp so I said, 'Good morning Moses,' and he replied, 'Good morning Pastor Barnabas,' so I started to check his memory and found it had been completely restored by this one long sleep. I thought it was right to have him checked medically, so Dr Daniel came and found to his astonishment that he was completely restored in mind and body.

Moses came back to Cambodia and he felt called to minister to the Laotians. His church today is halfway between Kong Kear's church and the Laotian border. The Lord found him a new wife who is very loving and caring and the church is growing in the village of Vaing Muong. Pastor Kong Kear helps him as the other churches in that area sprang up at the same time. Moses is now a nurse, so he does home visits, and preaches the gospel. His church cooks lunch for the primary school students.

These two churches are now linked with a Thai church pastor who came to Cambodia with a desire to help children in primary school. The building is used as a school and the vision was helped by the Thai pastor who had compassion for children. They walk long distances to school from the forests and paddyfields and often miss lunch because their parents do not have the money to feed them. I look afresh at how beautiful the Lord is and how lovely are his plans to meet the needs of these children from Laos, providing them with food, education and the Christian message. These Laotian children, taught the Christian faith by Pastor Moses, may well be instruments of blessing to communist Laos in the future.

Manit

Manit lived with her mother, sister and brother, after her father had left her mother for another woman. She was the eldest. She met a young man called Sothear, who was a believer and she married him. He shared his faith with the rest of the family and they all accepted the Lord. In the camp where I met Manit and Sothear in 1985, when my family came to Site Two, they spoke Thai and English as well as Cambodian and they worked for the Thai Red Cross. Their medical help was unique and done so beautifully that I invited them to come to my church. Afterwards they asked me not just to be their mentor but also their father. I trained them through the discipleship course.

Sothear was a brilliant man and I appointed him as my administrator. He was a faithful man who took great care of everything he did and his ability to look after finance was outstanding. He exemplified the teaching of the Lord in Luke 12:42: 'Who then is the faithful and wise manager, whom the master puts in charge of his servants to give them their food allowance at the proper time? It will be good for that servant whom the master finds doing so when he returns. I tell you the truth, he will put him in charge of all his possessions.' Sothear took all the teachings of Christ seriously, and put them into practice in his work. He saved me a lot of money by his expertly run financial management.

When we all returned to Phnom Penh, this couple and their mother in law settled in Kompong Cham near Battambang. This is the third largest city in Cambodia situated on the National Route 5. Sothear got a job with a non-government organisation with a good salary. Aware of the great need at that time to spread the message, he released his wife to serve the Lord full time; so Manit came to Phnom Penh to study the Bible with me. She was attending a house church called Peace Church, which focused on praising the Lord with music and regular meetings for prayer.

Returning to Battambang with Sothear they took into their care several young men who were left orphans by the Khmer Rouge years. They nurtured these orphans in the faith and Manit became the leading influence in that place. This was a change from the usual tradition of women never having any place at all. Their church was used as a catalyst in bringing other churches together. Manit organises seminars and pastors' conferences which I sometimes attend. Now there are over a hundred churches in the Battambang area.

Manit and Sothear had a daughter who loved the Lord very much when she was small but when she reached her teen years she went through a rebellious stage. It distressed her parents so much that Manit asked me for advice. This teenager behaved more like a man than a woman and she purchased many secular music CDs that contributed to her behaviour deteriorating even further. Manit's daughter and my daughter, Shalom had played together for eight years in Site Two camp and were good friends in those days. As I took this matter to the Lord, he revealed to me one night that it would be good for Shalom to renew her friendship with Manit's daughter.

So we arranged for them to share their school holidays together and trust the Lord to do a miracle to change that way of life. Shalom was such a great gift, she was a counsellor in her young years. As these two girls shared a room, their friendship was renewed and afterwards Manit's daughter returned home. A month later, I received a phone call from Manit. She had been astonished to watch her daughter becoming more and more feminine, and then she took all the secular CDs and buried them in the garden. Both parents praised the Lord for bringing this miracle about because Manit's daughter is a girl of great influence. She began speaking to many other girls in her home town and led them to the Lord. The result of all this was that Manit was able to send three other young people to attend our Institute of Church Planting. They all returned to their home towns to help their senior pastors.

This Battambang church has planted another church at the Thai border because one of the young people they had cared for got a job there. That family brought so much to that little town on the Thai border; they brought not just the Bible, not just the joy and hope that they found in Christ Jesus, but abundant life that surprised everyone living near them and also in their place of work. With the sound administration work of Sothear and help from our Bible Institute they have been able to build good churches for about US$500. These churches built of bamboo and thatch seat 60 people and they continue to grow today.

Just before I came to England in 2003 for the Keswick Convention, I received a phone call at nine o'clock in the morning from Manit who was in tears. She told me her husband had just been killed in a car accident so I made the journey there immediately. They asked me to officiate at the funeral service.

Barnabas wiped the tears that ran down his face as he recalled this tragedy. It was clearly a personal loss for him too. Resuming his composure he said:

About four hundred believers attended the funeral service and it struck the town people with awe. 'Why do so many attend a funeral service and what sort of people are these who love one another so much?' The police officer of the town attended and he admired the Christians' love.

Manit continues to serve the Lord and care for her three children. All are a special gift from the Lord and the eldest girl is admired by everyone, the second, a boy is so gifted, he could play the keyboard at the church when he was only eight years old. Now he leads the worship, and his elder sister plays the guitar; while the youngest, who is seven years old, is the organiser of the family. She reminds everyone of the time to do their duties in the home, their prayer time and the reading of the Bible. To be a shepherd and an equipper requires understanding of the importance of the father-daughter relationship. This family taught me much, and we have such strong bonds of love between us.

In Cambodia there is no problem of gender even though we came out of a Hinduistic tradition where women are ill-treated by men. It was first brought to Cambodia by the first king, Kaudimya Varman. Buddhism came to our country in the eighth century and it was accepted in the nation until the Killing Fields. More men were killed and far more women survived which necessitated them being the head of the family. A mother has to play two roles, a provider and manager of the home. Some women are in the leadership of the church, and Manit is one of them today, and she is accepted. I thank God that the church in Cambodia does not fight or argue over this issue. She helped me a lot in the camp as she is a talented singer. I made recordings of Cambodian hymns in a studio made of blankets, mud and hay. These recordings were used to bless the Cambodian church worldwide.

The father-daughter relationship is so important and so precious. Manit had no father after he left the family for another woman; so she regarded me as her spiritual father. I made one visit to this church and was so tired after the journey; she ministered to me and took great care of me. During that visit her father who had left her as a child came to see her for the first time. She said to him, 'Eight years ago when I was in Site Two camp I had no father, I never saw you until today. Because this pastor has loved me and cared for my family I can now gladly and freely forgive you for leaving me all those years ago.' The father knelt down and said 'thank you' to me so I learnt the reward of being a pastor and a father, not just to be loved by the church but to be accepted by their families as well. Manit continues to be a great leader in those churches and despite our gender bias background we are seeing and accepting that women who are called by the Lord can be effective in his kingdom.

CHAPTER TEN:

Cambodian Gemstones

Barnabas continued:

Sophal

Sophal joined the Khmer Rouge when he was only a boy, but after a short time he lost an arm in a battle. Everyone called him a one-armed bandit so he fled the country and came to Site Two camp where he fell in love with a beautiful girl who sold gold in the market place. To impress her, he joined the army again, but this time it was the resistance group that belonged to the coalition government. He asked the girl for her hand in marriage and she accepted. After they were married Sophal changed the course of his life by giving up the army altogether and he looked for a job. He attended a nursing class, qualified, then continued and finally became a medic. He worked in the camp hospital and came to our church where he found Christ.

He came to have a talk with me and felt guilty that he had married the girl really because she was well off and could earn a good income. He thought this was a safeguard as having only one arm, he might have a problem finding employment. I advised him to confess this to his wife and then the Lord would take care of them and he would also find a job. He was able to find a good job as a medic in the Site Two North camp hospital.

I lost track of him for some time as the camp was divided into Site Two North and Site Two South. I lived in Site Two South and he lived in Site Two North. There was a checkpoint between the two sites manned by the Thai military. We were not allowed to cross the checkpoints except on Sunday, but I thank God that as the church in the camp grew so did the grant from a Catholic organisation who were helping in relief, assistance and education. With money from that grant I was able to establish Hope English School.

We were running the church and the school which was so important for the future of the refugees. I also began a counselling course for the nurses and medics at the hospital. It was through this link that I met Sophal again and trained him in Bible teaching along with 50 others. Eventually he returned in 1993 with his family and settled in Kampot Province by the sea. There are large areas of salt flats in Kampot Province and Sophal and his wife took a house near one of the salt flats. They met with a small gathering of believers in their home; then the local authority encouraged them to seek permission of the department of religion to meet, so he applied but they insisted he join the denomination in his town. He was not informed about the variants of doctrine so he joined the Seventh Day Adventist church.

His beautiful wife couldn't read or write but she was very good at making money. This time she started raising pigs. It was a huge success but it offended the Adventist minister! Finally they quit the church but they were so lonely Sophal made the journey to Phnom Penh to see me. He had no idea where I lived but as he walked along the busy city roads he prayed, 'Lord, lead me to Barnabas.' Then he saw my wife in the market-place, and she brought him home. We were living in the small apartment that you visited in 1993 where we had a small church in the front room.

He shared with me the lack of joy, the problem of poor Bible teaching and all the rules and regulations that drove him mad! He pleaded with me to come and visit his family so I travelled to this town near the sea and the road was really bad. It took a long time to get there but I met the Adventist minister who knew me. We had a profitable conversation and he amicably agreed for Sophal to leave his church with no quarrel or fighting, and begin an evangelical one in that town. God used Sophal to share Christ's love with the people and to continue his career as a doctor. His home became a clinic and many came who didn't have any money to pay, but they still received help from him. Then he had difficulty in getting the needed medicines.

Living in Phnom Penh was an American who had been a pastor but left the ministry to care for the sick. He worked in a children's hospital that was supported by an American Christian agency. One of Sophal's patients, a little boy, became seriously ill and was admitted to this hospital where this former pastor worked as a doctor. Meeting Sophal he was impressed with his skill and offered him a job in the hospital. He stayed there for a while, and then I advised him to go back to his town, continue his medical work and remain in leadership of the church. The American agency agreed to supply him with free medicines and also train some of the church people in First Aid.

I continued to help Sophal in the church ministry placing elders in the fellowship to assist him. On the first harvest festival some folk from a Malaysian church in Kuala Lumpur made a visit, and the pastor preached. Thirty made a decision to follow Christ, and they have begun to attend Sophal's church. This is a different model of church growth because it grew initially by reaching out to the sick. Sophal has a monthly meeting with all the other Christians in that area so when I go to speak I reach some 40 churches. He is able to send out other church members into the villages with First Aid and the Christian message. There are groups now in all these villages, meeting in their homes as they did in the early chapters of the book of Acts. Sophal's church is known for its beautiful worship as he sent two of his daughters to Phnom Penh to learn to play the guitar and lead worship. They are both gifted musicians so this has enriched the church. It is a happy church with a one-armed pastor-doctor who cares for the spiritual and physical needs of all who come to be saved.

Uon Seila

While I was still in Site Two camp, Peter Davies of YWAM, who had a wonderful ministry in the camp to the refugees, introduced me to a Cambodian refugee who had a long, sad face. No one could cheer him up. As I befriended this man I discovered his wife had left him because she did not want to look after their little son. He was broken-hearted that she had left, saying she would never return and he must care for the little boy. I asked Peter more about the man and found that he was helping in the hospital and was highly intelligent. Peter and I came alongside him and showed him the love of Christ. He made a full commitment to follow Jesus and decided to change his name to Seila (in Cambodian this word means Cephas or rock) connecting it with Peter whose faith was as strong as a rock. After he had been so broken about the loss of his wife he felt he needed to harden a little! Finally Seila made a decision to be baptised.

I had the responsibility of being the director of the Campus Crusade for Christ ministry in Site Two camp.

Sothear, Manit's husband, was my administrator but I needed more pillars to help. Seila told me he was working for YWAM, but seeing his ability I decided to approach my good friend Phil Scott to see if I could have Seila to help me. They were so kind and allowed him to come and help.

Now Seila is a very talented writer and he was equally good in business studies. After he was baptised his faith grew stronger every day. He is not an eloquent preacher but his writings are very thought-provoking. He told me he felt the love of Jesus had helped him to overcome the severe depression he suffered after his wife left him. He took some Bible studies in the camp and he developed a unique gift in writing. We found we were birds of a feather because I love writing and literature. I mentored Seila and encouraged him to use these gifts to edify new Christians in the camp. Every leader should observe those with talent and allow them to exercise these gifts for kingdom growth.

We worked together for two years and I found he was also a musician. So with the help of World Vision, I gave him a twelve-stringed guitar. In the camp we had no hymn books but just memorised songs for worship. With Seila's gifts we put together a small hymn book of about 40 songs of praise and worship which were used in the camp meetings. Seila knew how to use a computer so he was able to put these songs and music together and we had our first song book in 1990. This was rather late, but better late than never!

In God's grace and goodness Seila married a younger, beautiful and supportive wife and we all returned to Phnom Penh in 1993. He asked if he could join me in the building of a church in the city. I had no church at that time so I introduced him to one of the growing churches in Phnom Penh where he became one of the elders, and YWAM again gave him a job.

The president of World Vision in America made a visit to Phnom Penh and interviewed me. Two donors came at the same time and were impressed with the concept of us nationals preaching alongside the projects as this was being used of God to help the church grow. They were prepared to put a large sum of money into propagating the gospel throughout Cambodia. The expatriate workers had certain restrictions on them at that time but as a national these did not apply to me. I began to preach the gospel alongside some of the projects of World Vision to help with the great needs of the poor. There was a call for a Leadership Consultation and all the elders of the national churches that were in existence met together with World Vision. The outcome was a decision to start a project called Training of Timothys and the funds were there for us to spread the message far and wide throughout Cambodia as the Lord helped us to develop suitable candidates. We lacked the number of people who were firm enough in the word so I asked Seila to help me as project manager and YWAM were doubly gracious and released him again, so that he could help me.

Seila's calling was not with pastors but with young people. He had written a number of articles that had new parables in Khmer culture to illustrate the Kingdom concept so God is using him to bring young people to Christ through his writings. He was asked by the EFC to become a co-director of their Youth Commission along with Brian Maher. They work together really well and everyone has great respect for Brian as he has had a heart for the Cambodian people for many years working with World Vision. Seila has made a good contribution as he is always full of new ideas for the young people.

When the Youth Conference (organised by the EFC) took place in Kompong Som (or Sihanoukville) in the year 2000, I spoke on the book of Ruth for the young women and afterwards on Boaz for the young men. I helped them to see Ruth as the church of the gentiles and Boaz as a type of Christ. Revd Heng Cheng spoke about God's design for marriage. We laid down strong biblical concepts of purity in behaviour and told the assembled young people of the necessity of safe sex within the marriage bond and sanctity without. This is so necessary in our society. The Youth Commission has been very successful in teaching hundreds of young people the whole counsel of God so they become strong in the faith for the church of tomorrow. The youth camps are held annually and I have given the opening address every year. I asked to be relieved from this but Brian and Seila have said I must finish in my tenth year so there are two more years to go.

Paul says, 'I have not hesitated to proclaim to you the whole will of God' (NIV) see Acts 20:27 so we must do the same and that counsel is physical, spiritual, material, financial and social. So I see Seila who lost his first wife, touched by God in Site Two camp, equipped by the suffering to be an effective worker for the youth of Cambodia. Seila is also a poet who composes verses and sets them to music for the young people so God has been so good to us to gift the growing church with such men.

Brom Sambo

In the English classes taught in Site Two camp there were officers of quite high rank. One of these student officers was very keen to learn English but not interested in being a Christian. His name was Brom Sambo and he was working with a mother and child health clinic which was part of the work of Christian Outreach. Sambo finished the English course and he did well, but I was concerned to see him become a Christian. I shared my desire with the British leaders of Christian Outreach who are spiritually minded, so they prayed for him as well. Then someone told me that he was attending a sister church of mine, so I was pleased, but I was even more pleased when I was told he had made a commitment to Christ. Christian Outreach moved him on to work as their health staff manager.

Sambo and his family returned to Phnom Penh and he started to look for a job, and found one with Food for the Hungry who shared offices with Christian Outreach. God used this job to strengthen him in the faith and he ultimately became one of the leaders of Food for the Hungry.

In 1994 Phnom Penh was not a safe place but some of the provincial towns where some of the converts from Site Two camp settled, were even more dangerous. The government had not been firmly established and everyone did as they pleased. There was no safety with the police as they did their job from early morning until midday and after that it was every man for himself.

Food for the Hungry was working in one of these provincial towns in Chook District when one of their workers, Melissa Himes, was kidnapped. This made world headlines but God protected her; she was eventually released unharmed. Sambo who was one of the reluctant converts from my English class in Site Two camp was a project manager for FFTH and he was growing in the faith. Paul of Cambodia and I started to preach alongside the projects of FFTH and many people made a commitment to Christ so we helped set up a small house church, which we mentored and put in place good structures to ensure sound foundations for the church. Sometimes we stayed over weekends and came back during the week to Phnom Penh.

Yet as the Christian message took root in the lives of new converts, God performed miracles of healing and arranged extraordinary acts of protection. During a Sunday service in this small church that was held in the front room of a little apartment, five soldiers suddenly burst into the meeting threatening everyone with their guns. Something stopped them in their tracks and they sat down to listen instead of killing us. At the end of that service all five of them knelt down and confessed their sins and made a commitment to Christ.

A former police officer was badly injured in a road accident and lost most of his sight. We prayed for his full restoration and he received perfect vision. In fact, he rode his motorbike round the city streets shouting, 'I can see, I can see everything, Jesus has healed me!' Quite a crowd came to the church from the market area that heard this man shouting on his bike and they all became Christians. A lady who had had surgery on her larynx lost her voice completely. She came to the little church and after prayer she shouted the name of Jesus to everyone. After seeing the Lord do all these great things Paul and I decided to return to Phnom Penh late one evening.

We said goodbye to the little church and started the long journey home. On the way we were accosted by three robbers with bazookas. One was standing in front of our truck and two were behind. They were looking for any valuables such as watches or cameras to steal and we had some good cameras with us so I prayed, 'Lord, please save us from these wicked men.' Then I heard him saying there is power in praise! So we started singing praise songs and the robbers stopped threatening us; their leader shouted, 'We mustn't hurt singers, they are just singers so let's leave them alone.' We thanked the Lord for his powerful protection and arrived in Phnom Penh safely. There is now a fellowship of 18 churches in that area which resulted from a reluctant convert from the English class in Site Two camp.

So we can see how God used the dark years when Cambodians were forced to go to the refugee camps to survive. These refugee trained Christians had fanned out from the capital city and gone to provinces throughout the country to take the message of salvation and help the local people in their times of need. Sambo finally encountered Jesus in the camp, so he was compelled by the love of Christ, sent out in his power even though he was not properly equipped in doctrine and theology. He ministered to their social needs and then introduced them to the gospel.

These are stories of God's intervention in the lives of ordinary men and women, who walked through fiery furnaces of affliction; these were jewels in the making to be used by him for his great purposes in the land of Cambodia.

CHAPTER ELEVEN:

One who stayed behind:
Paul of Cambodia

Paul is one of the few surviving Christians who remained in the country throughout the dark years under Pol Pot and the Vietnamese. He has a quiet demeanour, is a little shy and has a good sense of humour. When he began to tell about his experiences his face lit up.

Paul was born in Phnom Penh into a Buddhist family, going to the pagodas, listening to the monks and observing the holy days. During the early sixties, the education system was the best it ever was and his father and mother both had good jobs. He attended high school and heard the students discussing a crusade with Dr Stanley Mooneyham. Paul decided to go to the Bassac Theatre on the river front where he heard the evangelist and decided to follow Christ. Many who made a commitment to Christ at the Mooneyham crusades went on to become catalysts for an evangelism explosion that lasted until April 1975 when Pol Pot came to power. Those converts, like Paul, were also instrumental in carrying on the work of the underground church in the eighties and initiated church planting and training of leaders in the nineties. He told me that for several years he did not fully commit his life to the Lord while he was a law student in the University of Phnom Penh and his education came to a halt when the Khmer Rouge took the city.

In 1975 when the city-dwellers were ordered to leave, he joined the exodus with his family. He was only twenty when they were forced to live in a village and were split up into different labour forces. Two of his sisters were killed as slave labourers. There were many families from the city living in this village and nearly all of them were killed. Pol Pot's intention was to kill all the country's intelligentsia. Despite their obvious education, in God's ways the rest of Paul's family were saved. This was the first miracle they experienced and it was this evidence of a God who had protected him that made him start his Christian life in earnest.

The Khmer Rouge cadre in charge of the slave labourers was cruel and tried unsuccessfully to catch him and his family doing something wrong. Paul was frequently taken for interrogation but he maintained the truth in all he said and survived many dangerous situations. The Khmer Rouge leader read out lists of names each evening and those on the lists disappeared, later to be discovered in mass graves. Others died of disease and starvation. But Paul and his family remained miraculously untouched by the angel of death. During the years of exile in the village, he was frequently exhausted by 20-hour days building dykes and canals in the hot sun with only one bowl of rice gruel a day. It was God's divine protection that reaffirmed Paul's initial faith in the God of the Bible.

Eventually the Khmer Rouge was ousted by the Vietnamese army and Paul with the remains of his family returned to Phnom Penh where his father obtained a job with World Vision at the National Paediatric Hospital. Paul remembers his first Christmas being celebrated in a house where he met up with Barnabas and others who were part of the underground church.

There was no freedom to worship and Barnabas was being watched by the communists. The church began with only 30 people but it grew in the shadows to nearly two hundred. During that period they worshipped together with the Roman Catholics, and it was a place of love and caring for each other. They were untainted by denominationalism and although they had to change their venue frequently as there was no freedom to meet together from the authorities, they were bound together in the bonds of Christ and the fact that they had survived the Killing Fields era.

In 1984 this nucleus of believers was betrayed to the government by one of their own members. Real problems arose the following year when, under the threat of his life, Barnabas fled to Thailand. Paul's name had been on the wanted list but no government official knew his face so he survived under a variety of different names. Another key worker in the underground church was Timothy but he was arrested and taken for interrogation. After that incident Timothy with the help of Paul escaped to the Thai border and found Barnabas in the Site Two camp. Timothy was able to go to the States as a refugee but Paul remained in the camp only a few weeks. He had married a Cambodian girl who was still in Phnom Penh so he was constantly thinking of her. Working as a nurse in the camp hospital was a Swiss girl who kept him in the faith. Through a secret grapevine she told Paul that his wife was expecting a baby so he made a risky decision to return to Phnom Penh.

On the hazardous journey, he lived with terrible fear but was absolutely convinced that God had called him to return to Phnom Penh. Although the Vietnamese had taken over from the Khmer Rouge, fighting continued and there were more privations to endure under Vietnamese rule. Passing through mined fields, soldiers fired at him, mortar bombs exploded over his head. He recalled with amazement one incident when God had clearly made him invisible when he tried to cross a river. There were armed soldiers with guns ready to fire, but he was certain that God had made them unable to see him. On this dangerous journey he had nine other companions who felt they must return to the city. He was arrested by a Khmer Rouge soldier but after careful questioning he let him go. In terrible fear he and his companions discovered they were walking through a mined field. One of the little group was a qualified de-miner so he went ahead of them to secure their safety. Paul had one experience after another of amazing deliverance that could only have been the protection of an Almighty, all-powerful God. After months of this terrifying journey he had only one sign of injury: his feet were torn and bleeding with the thorns he had trodden on.

Finally he reached Phnom Penh and found his wife; only ten days later she gave birth to a son, which he felt was yet another amazing blessing from God. He resumed meeting with the underground church and began teaching and discreetly evangelising. This led to planting about nine other churches in the city, and all were survivors of the Killing Fields, but there was no freedom to meet openly. So it was not without reason that these persecuted Christians had something in common with the early church under the leadership of Paul, Barnabas and Timothy.

After Timothy left, Barnabas' life was threatened too and he was arrested; years of hardship and prison life followed before he reached Site Two camp, leaving Paul to continue the church leadership in Phnom Penh. He was involved in all aspects of the church during the eighties when they were forced to meet in secret as Cambodians were considered treasonous if found to be embracing the Christian faith. They had leadership seminars, showed the *Jesus* film in a room with black covers over the windows, and quietly listened to FEBC Radio.

Despite the restrictions Paul planted churches in three provinces and after 1993 he became part of 'Every Home for Christ' which does a lot of literature distribution and encourages small groups to meet in homes. Paul was instrumental in nurturing the spiritual life of the underground church in the eighties and he was the main founder of the Evangelical Fellowship of Cambodia, serving three consecutive terms as chairman of the board and also president of the Cambodian Bible Society.

Asking Paul why the church had grown so rapidly he replied that the Christian message in Cambodia is hope to a hopeless people. The intervention of western missionaries had played a significant part, but in the early years he was disturbed and angry at the number of missionaries who offered existing church members a good salary if they joined their particular denomination. The underground church had known nothing about denominations, but it was a fellowship of love for one another, and it had included some Vietnamese Christians. Denominationalism and inappropriate missions sadly divided the believers and brought with them jealousies and rivalry.

The present freedom to worship had given impetus to the growing hunger for righteousness and salvation that is on the increase in this nation. His concern was that the church is still one of young believers who need to grow in the faith, but to help them grow they need to read good literature and hear good radio programmes. FEBC were now broadcasting in Cambodia but a publishing house for Christian literature was the greatest need. I talked with Paul on this issue as I had had a burden in August 2003 to find help for a publishing house to be set up in Cambodia. He confirmed this need and said there was no lack of good Khmer writers.

Paul feared that the children of Cambodia today have no knowledge of the Killing Fields era: they regard it as just a story. The huge lack of education and books needs to be addressed, if the church is to grow to maturity. He felt his own gifts were in the field of discipling others rather than in leading a church. He had also been involved in Vietnam in teaching the underground church. This was done with great sensitivity in order to protect the local Christians. I discovered he had been to the church where I had supplied Bibles.

Paul says there is a hunger for righteousness in the nation now that has never been there before and this is because they know the moral standard of their lives has been bad, and they long for something to build them up spiritually. The teachings of the Bible are the only source that will satisfy that hunger and bring the nation to righteousness. They have passed through the monarchist system, to the republican, to communism, to socialist and now democracy, fragile though it is. He laughed at 'democracy' and said it should be renamed semi-democracy! The Paris Peace Accord had clearly stated that the people had a right to believe in Christianity, so that gave impetus to the growing church. It was a fitting ending to a memorable morning to have lunch with Paul and talk about our common interest in Vietnam. This deeply spiritual man is quiet, unassuming but has a burning desire to use every moment of his life in service to the Master in a behind-the-scenes role.

Pastor Barnabas says there are four harvest forces helping to rebuild the church of Christ and help the nation: Christians who stayed in Cambodia throughout the terrible years; those who left the refugee camps and settled in a western country and were converted there; and those who went to the refugee camps and were exposed to western culture but were not immersed in it. The fourth force is the western missions who are planting churches. Some are inappropriate to the culture in Cambodia while others recognise the place that the nationals have in preaching and caring. Only as these harvest forces unite and work together will the church continue to grow and be a force for good in Cambodia.

CHAPTER TWELVE:

A Leader of Consequence:
Heng Cheng

The Evangelical Fellowship of Cambodia (EFC) has clearly had great influence in the growth of the church and Revd Heng Cheng is the General Secretary. Spending a morning with this leader and his wife Sandar was a privilege for me. His own pathway to faith was fraught with difficulties from childhood. He was born into a Christian family in Kompot Province in 1947, an only child of a Chinese father and a Cambodian–Chinese mother. His father had come from a strong Christian background in China, but they all had to leave their homeland because of the fighting towards the end of World War Two.

Settling in Cambodia, his father married a Cambodian lady who was not a Christian. When Cheng was only one month old his father quarrelled with the rest of his family, (probably over his marriage which they strongly disapproved of) and left to work as a stevedore on the dockside of the Bassac River. His mother, who was left alone to look after him, died when he was three months old. Having no interest at all in his little son, his father sold him to a Vietnamese man who raised him for a year.

Then a Cambodian government official asked to adopt Cheng. He did adopt him and brought him to Phnom Penh. His father told his brother that Cheng was now in

Revd Heng Cheng and his wife Sandar

Phnom Penh with the government official's family. Two years later Cheng's uncle asked to have him back and bring him up with his family! The uncle succeeded but he already had five children of his own. Cheng wasn't told that his uncle and aunt were not his real parents as they kept this a secret. In 1965 his uncle died and his adopted mother died eight years later. As she was dying she told Cheng the truth about his real parents, and the fact that his natural father had asked about him from time to time but he had remarried and had four children by his second wife. His real father died in the Pol Pot years and his children all fled the country and were resettled in Australia. It was a stormy, difficult childhood yet God had his plans for this young man. In spite of all the circumstances, he did well at school and wanted to become a doctor.

As a boy he remembers worshipping in a church that was planted by missionary David Ellison in the 1960s. He had a good education but lacked the money to go to university, so joined the forces serving in Lon Nol's

American-backed army who were fighting against the Viet Cong and the Khmer Rouge. He was a man with outstanding leadership qualities and was Captain of the Mike Force. This elite force rode around in trucks with signs pasted on their sides, 'Tomorrow we die'. He sustained an injury in the army and was sick of fighting, so quitting the army he contacted his eldest cousin who wanted to help him. He began studying medicine at the Faculty of Medicine in Phnom Penh; making contact with his natural father during that period wasn't a success because he had no feelings towards his son so Cheng felt unable to continue any relationship with him because of his bitterness over his father's rejection.

His medical studies were interrupted by the Pol Pot regime; being educated they wanted to kill him so he fled to Vietnam in 1976. He was arrested in Vietnam and given a short prison sentence as they thought he was a Khmer Rouge supporter. When the charges against him were found to be false he was released. Earning a living by selling medicines he became involved with the political scene, helping people to leave communism and resettle in Taiwan, Hong Kong, Thailand and the Philippines. Living in Saigon was an aunt who was a Christian. She tried to lead him to the Lord, but Cheng was not sure he wanted to be a Christian so he attended the Catholic church sometimes and at other times he went with the Watch Tower people (Jehovah's Witnesses). In 1978 Cheng made a full commitment to the Lord and gradually backed out of his involvement with the politics associated with the civil war.

He regularly attended a CAMA church and during the troubles in Vietnam, CAMA arranged an underground Bible school which he attended. It was a dangerous thing to do but he was prepared for adversity. They were very inventive about venues, which were frequently changed to avoid detection by the communists. Classes were held on a bus, on a boat on the river, sometimes this church and sometimes that church. They had classes in the city and classes in the country; Heng Cheng attended all these and in 1981 he became a youth pastor in a CAMA church in Saigon.

He married his lovely Vietnamese wife and returned to Phnom Penh in 1985, and started a Cambodian–Vietnamese church that would later be called the New Jerusalem Church. It came under the Assemblies of God and he helped train church leadership, followed up on new believers, took care of church administration and visited the sick. No one paid much attention to this church and Heng Cheng was thought to be a Vietnamese spy by the other Christians.

In 1993 Cheng gave testimony at Global Network when Cambodian Christian Services (the predecessor of EFC) were preparing a March for Jesus. During the planning meeting Cheng stood and made a fiery speech about the lack of unity in the Christian community and how he had been ostracised because of unfounded suspicions and prejudice. He recited Revelation 5:9,10 to the assembled Christian leaders. '"You are worthy to take the scroll and to open its seals, because you were slain, and with your blood you purchased men for God from every tribe and language and people and nation. You have made them to be a kingdom and priests to serve our God, and they will reign on the earth."' Then he said, 'You won't receive me and my church, but the blood of Christ purchased me and my people and added us into a group from every tribe and tongue. If you won't accept us we aren't going to lose sleep over it. Jesus has already accepted us and we are already a part of a much bigger community than yours. Have it your way if you think you must.'

After Cheng's powerful and moving testimony, those who attended this meeting saw tears in the eyes of

Barnabas Mam who had felt Heng Cheng's pain at the way he was being rejected by fellow Christians. By the end of the meeting it was decided that the Jerusalem Church was to be responsible for the worship in the first March for Jesus in 1994. In late 1996 the new-born Evangelical Fellowship of Cambodia invited Heng Cheng to become the general secretary. He resigned from his leadership role in the Jerusalem Church to take up full-time responsibility in the EFC.

During the time I had with this inspiring leader he told me how he had safeguarded the EFC against a suggested takeover by the World Council of Churches. With his clear thinking and lack of compromise he has helped to keep freedom for the churches that are members of the EFC; to evangelise everyone in the country whatever their religious background. In talks with the World Peace Religious Council he was able to steer the EFC into the right channels and yet at the same time to be a witness to many in high places.

The government has great respect for the EFC and Revd Heng Cheng has had really positive discussions with the prime minister. Through these talks he obtained permission for a Christian programme on Cambodian television and freedom to broadcast the gospel through radio outreaches all over the country. He said he would like to become a writer and use his vast experience to teach the younger generation of believers how to capture a full Christian world view in order to properly lead the church to transform Cambodian society.

On the mission front he concluded, 'Many foreign missionaries want to plant churches when the nationals are able to do it better. They have the right and freedom to do so, but it would be more effective and wiser for them to walk alongside the nationals and help them do it, rather than hiring a few translators and going out on their own.' The government has seen how the Christians have helped in many needy areas especially setting up good orphanages and helping with health issues. When EFC Christians build a church they get planning permission and then ask the prime minister to come to the official opening! Imagine us being able to do that in so-called Christian England!

After 1993 the government were taking the need for a democratic system seriously so through a friendship with a high-ranking official, Revd Heng Cheng was able to obtain freedom for several radio stations, FEBC and Trans World Radio are just two known to me. Revd Heng Cheng made a point of telling these influential men (high-ranking government officials) that the EFC prays for them regularly. They replied that even the Buddhists don't do this for them! There are now eight hours of Christian radio; New Life, FEBC and Trans World Radio all having their own channels. In 2000, Revd Heng Cheng, Barnabas and Paul met with King Sihanouk at the Cambodiana Hotel and they had a most helpful time together and have obtained written permission for great freedom for all the Christians to evangelise the country.

Revd Heng Cheng meets with King Sihanouk on his birthday each year to have a time of prayer with him. The leaders of EFC also have meetings with the prime minister and pray for him. He told me they have established a good friendship with both and it is mutually appreciated by the King and Hun Sen. When Revd Heng Cheng goes out into the provinces for preaching and teaching seminars with the local churches he always invites the provincial government minister to have dinner with him afterwards. After a good dinner he then introduces him to the local church leader, so that they work together for the good of the church. Smiling warmly, he said, 'We have had more trouble with a leader of the Nazarene Church who wanted to control the whole church in Cambodia! I am on his blacklist because he has made a lot of difficulties for us.'

In some rural areas the government officials are still communistic in their thinking and they do oppose church building and evangelising. There was strong opposition in Stung Treng and a lot of problems with a government official; so Cheng went personally with other leaders of EFC and spoke at length with the opposing official. There was disunity among the Christians as well but after discussions and a seminar, all came together and established a good relationship with the local government official that has facilitated church growth and mutual respect for one another.

Out of the hard times Revd Heng Cheng has acquired wisdom and resources of integrity that are needed in the growth of the church. Job 28:12–18 says, '"But where can wisdom be found? Where does understanding dwell? Man does not comprehend its worth; it cannot be found in the land of the living. The deep says, 'It is not in me'; the sea says, 'It is not with me.' It cannot be bought with the finest gold, nor can its price be weighed in silver. It cannot be bought with the gold of Ophir, with precious onyx or sapphires. Neither gold nor crystal can compare with it, nor can it be had for jewels of gold. Coral and jasper are not worthy of mention; the price of wisdom is beyond rubies."' It was through intense suffering that Job found wisdom to write those words and God knew that Heng Cheng would be a leader of consequence in Cambodia because he had been through many hardships and learnt to fear God. 'The fear of the Lord – that is wisdom' (Job 28:28).

CHAPTER THIRTEEN:

Forgiving the Past:
Sokreaksa Himm

It is generally known that Cambodians celebrate an annual Day of Hate in order to keep their hatred towards the Khmer Rouge on the boil. As there is so little justice in the courts a lot of people do resort to shooting one another in revenge attacks. These 'ghosts from the past' sometimes invade the church with dissensions and disunity but there has been one example of forgiving that has led to churches being planted.

I met Sokreaksa Himm when he came to England in 2003 for the launch of his book *The Tears of My Soul*. (In this book you can read Reaksa's own story of how God called him to return to his home area after his family was killed by the Khmer Rouge. Published by Monarch, 2003.) He stayed at our home with his wife Sophaly and little son Philos.

Reaksa was only thirteen years old when his parents, brothers and sisters were clubbed to death and thrown into an open grave. He was badly hurt by one of the murderers but regained consciousness at the end of the day. Crawling over the bodies of his family he got out of the grave and wandered about in a state of severe shock. After many years of turmoil, feelings of revenge, hopelessness and fear, he finally resettled in Canada where he met Jesus as his Saviour. Using his considerable intellectual skills he qualified in Theology and then made the costly decision to return to Cambodia to help his fellow countrymen and women to overcome their traumas and learn about the Christian faith. Settling into the area where his family lay buried, he met with the family killers and told them how he was able to forgive them through knowing forgiveness from Jesus Christ. He was able to tell them that before he became a Christian he was filled with anger, resentment and a desire for revenge. Through receiving Christ's forgiveness he was now able to forgive them for killing his family. He has one surviving sister.

Reaksa's book makes riveting reading but his subsequent actions have shown that to obey and put into practise the Lord's teaching to forgive can have a remarkable effect.

In November 2003 I flew to Siem Reap to meet Sokreaksa Himm and his family. Reaksa took me to the little church he had helped to establish near the village of Pouk where his sister still lives in the family home. Reaksa wisely refrained from telling me there was no road access to the church from his sister's house. He had arranged for his nephew to give me a lift from the house on a motorbike! I am terrified of motorbikes but had to overcome my fears and respect the Cambodian tradition of women sitting side-saddle on a motorbike. So I held on to the rider's seat as we rode slowly through a lightly wooded area, I noticed there were giant black butterflies with white 'eyes' on their wings, and some other fearful-looking insects. I was relieved when the little church building in the wooded clearing came into sight.

Reaksa introduced me to Pastor Vansan Hong. He had a congregation of about 30 and a Sunday school was held outside under a shady tree. While visiting the church, a Buddhist funeral was taking place in a neighbouring

Pastor Vansan Hong

bamboo-thatch house. At funerals or weddings the Buddhist tradition is for the monks to chant loudly over amplifiers to cleanse the evil spirits from the house of the deceased. The church congregation sat on the floor and sang praise songs, a welcome sound contrasting with the nearby wailing. When the time came for the sermon it was quite remarkable that the monks took a break so the teaching was heard without competition.

Nearby, Reaksa had set up a chicken farm to help the new Christians earn a living. He had also taught them to plant and sell vegetables and provided a well for clean water. As the church had grown Reaksa was able to find a pastor who had studied in Phnom Penh to lead the church. Pastor Vansan, a former teacher, was a very genial, happy Christian and there was a real feeling of love and support between all the congregation. This small Cambodian church, planted in the area where Reaksa's family were clubbed to death and thrown into an open grave, is now a beacon of hope and the fruits of his forgiveness. People living there ask, why does this man who has lived in Canada forgive, what makes him love us so much? There are about 30 other little house groups meeting in the area for Bible study and singing praise songs.

A western couple arrived as the service was ending and Reaksa introduced me to them. Dan and Rose Brosser were working in Phnom Penh with Trans World Radio (TWR). TWR broadcast Bible teaching over the airwaves from their Cambodian base in Phnom Penh. I talked with Dan and Rose and told them how Trans World Radio had always had a special place in my heart because over 30 years ago I had tuned into their broadcasts when I was depressed after losing my family members who were an extreme separatist sect. I remembered writing to their studio in Monte Carlo and receiving a loving, encouraging letter in return from a lady called Nora Freed. The Brossers told me she was now in her nineties and still transmitting on the radio. TWR broadcast a variety of different programmes for all ages. They also provide follow-up for people who contact them to be put in touch with a local church. Additionally, they produce CDs of their teaching programmes and this is sent to small churches for their use in Bible studies.

The Brossers shared the view held by many that there is a strategic work being carried out in the freedom of Cambodia with communist Laos and Vietnam on its borders, and Muslim Malaysia and Indonesia in the south, all needing gospel outreach. This has been prepared by God and could yet be the vehicle of God's blessing in those lands. TWR programmes and those of the Far East Broadcasting Company (FEBC) who had been broadcasting longer, have contributed to the growth of the church. Khmers will listen to the radio and so the word of God on the airwaves and through the witness of God's people is bearing fruit throughout the country. Two young men in the province of Kampong Speu (south of Phnom Penh) heard some of the TWR programmes. They wanted to hear more about this Jesus. They travelled into Phnom Penh and found the TWR Office. 'Can you help us?' they asked. They were put in touch with a couple working in an orphanage near where they lived. As a result 14 people are meeting weekly in three different groups to study God's word.

It was a memorable day with Reaksa, his wife Sophaly and little Philos but especially a privilege to worship together in that little church that was representing the love and compassion of Jesus to a hurt and broken people. Indeed, Reaksa had a totally new idea for raising funds for the church support. He had about 70 baby crocodiles in a special enclosure in his garden. When they reached adult size he would sell them in the market as South Koreans eat the meat, the skins fetch a high price and Chinese people use the bones for medicinal purposes. Pastor Vansan fed and looked after the crocodiles until they were ready for market so he needed prayer support! Having observed pigs being taken to market in a basket on the back of a bicycle, I did wonder if the crocodiles would be taken in a similar manner!

A few months after this church service, Reaksa's brother-in-law was riding the motorbike to go to the Bible study one evening when robbers sprang out of the jungle area and shot him, stealing the motor bike. This awful event shook all the Christians and in the face of this further tragedy, Reaksa has had to come to terms with losing another loved relative and to express forgiveness for such a callous deed. No one has been charged with the murder. If forgiveness can be given after all the sufferings Reaksa has been through, how much more readily should we extend forgiveness to those who have treated us spitefully? We repeat the Lord's prayer: 'Forgive us our debts, as we also have forgiven our debtors' (Mt. 6:12). But do we put this into practise?

CHAPTER FOURTEEN:

Perseverance through Trials

While I was in Siem Reap I renewed my links with Marie, the professional jeweller and artist who had started the handicrafts project in Phnom Penh. After the murder in the office she had made a decision to move to Siem Reap and help the disadvantaged people in that area. Taking her little adopted Cambodian son Joseph with her she soon found a shop with a spacious flat over it and began to teach crafts to homeless young people in the town. The Cambodian people she had trained made beautiful jewellery and a wide variety of handicrafts. Marie told me that she employed some amputees in her handicraft project, and there were several other agencies offering similar help. Nevertheless, there are new victims every month from the numerous landmines that still litter the countryside.

We decided to spend the day together visiting the Tonle Sap lake and nearby Angkor Wat, the huge complex of ancient crumbling temples depicting heathen gods and dating back to the ninth and twelfth centuries. It is the main attraction for all the tourists who come in droves to the newly built luxurious hotels and we talked much of the challenges brought about by such a meeting of ancient civilisation with western culture and the implications for Christian mission.

The Angkor Wat complex covers about 60 square miles and shows the tremendous talent the Khmer people had in art, design, architecture and sculpture. The temples of Angkor Wat are magnificent in their architectural grandeur but there is a lesson from nature in these temple ruins. Over the centuries many of the temples have had their entrances slowly closed because trees have grown and spread their roots over the crumbling buildings. These remarkable trees are the strangler fig and the paler, thicker-limbed silk cotton tree (ceiba pentandra). A seed created by the great eternal God (dropped by birds centuries ago) sprouted and sent down roots into these buildings. As I observed these ancient temples, with these huge spreading trees that are now almost strangling the old places of worship, I marvelled at God's amazing creation. The seed planted hundreds of years ago is now a great tree with ever-spreading branches and long roots above the ground that are threatening to take over the temples as if to say, 'God is not living in these temples. Seek him through the temples of his Holy Spirit that are residing in this area in human vessels, with a message of forgiveness that leads to eternal life.' These Angkor Wat temples will fade away one day, but the human temples that are shining jewels in this once totally pagan area, will dance before the throne of God when they will be surpassed only by the presence of the King of Glory himself. He will dwell with these precious souls and will wipe away every tear.

The villagers close to this now thriving town watch the western tourists and have become very anti anything western as a result. They hear reports of child abuse, trafficking of women and babies, while paedophiles take advantage of unwanted homeless children. This has given them good cause to dislike westerners.

Staying in one of the tourist hotels I could understand this, as I observed westerners complaining, eating and drinking to excess – and the scant dress of many is offensive in Buddhist culture. Marie explained that as she set up some small groups for Bible study she made no attempt to bring in any western-style songs but taught only Khmer songs of praise set to Khmer music.

Some westerners with the best of motives had seen the dire poverty in the villages and gone to help with bags of rice and clothes, and afterwards invited them to join a church. The first question the village people ask is how much money will I get if I go to this church? Despite this inappropriate method, some were coming to know Jesus and follow him, but no lasting work could be done in this area without being culturally sensitive and getting alongside the people by building bridges of friendship. Marie was pleasantly surprised that some people had made a positive response in spite of a bad approach.

Christianity is a religion that is totally alien to Khmer people so there is need for loving relationships to be built in order to earn trust. This whole area was once ruled by Pol Pot and everyone was taught to instantly obey or they were killed, so there is still a fear and mistrust of one another if anyone conducts themselves in a different manner from the traditional ways of life. Marie starts to teach the people the book of Genesis and tells them about their Creator God, because Buddhism has no concept of a Creator. She then proceeds to teach through the Old Testament into the New, so they can see that their Saviour and Redeemer was there at the beginning with God the Father of humankind and the Creator of the world. Working with small groups, building friendships and holding parties with food at Christmas and Easter, she has been instrumental in adding many new members to an existing Khmer church in Siem Reap. This is a strong indigenous church that would survive if every westerner was thrown out of the country, as happened earlier in the history of this nation.

If missionaries start with just the teachings of Jesus, a Buddhist would question how someone younger than Buddha can help? In the village setting people will come together to hear the gospel, but their concentration level is low for two reasons. They are often very hungry and tired, and they are still suffering from the traumas they experienced in the Killing Fields. Marie felt that Reaksa's decision, for example, to come back to this part of Cambodia and help a Khmer pastor to build the church was a very positive thing to do. He understands how Khmer people think and also has sympathetic insight into the traumas they have been through.

Marie has worked for over six years with the Khmer staff she employs in her shop and the village people who are making the handicrafts, but she is still teaching them Christian values and ethics. The day starts in the shop with a Bible study and worship to the Lord. Some Khmer people have problems with honesty but this needs to be set in perspective because of so much poverty. Many Khmer people eat only one meal a day.

While Marie was working in the camp she was used by the Lord to bring many to know Christ. When they returned to their homeland some settled in Kirivong, and she helped them to establish a church in that town, which is near the Vietnamese border. A Khmer pastor leads, and the church has grown in numbers and strength. One of the members of that church is currently studying at Phnom Penh Bible School and will take up a leadership position when he has qualified.

Some of the tourists who go to Siem Reap for cheap sex and the exploitation of children know that very few of them will ever go before the courts. There has been a New Zealand man living in Siem Reap for ten years for this very reason, but the young girls he preys on are too scared to tell their mothers. If they do, the mothers sometimes won't admit that their daughter has been abused because she would not be regarded as fit for marriage in Khmer culture. Recently, as I am writing this, the New Zealand man was arrested because one mother had the courage to go and report him to the police. However, there is an English doctor in Phnom Penh, struck off the register by the British Medical Council for child abuse, but who has practised medicine in the city for a long time.

On a positive note, Marie has trained women from the church in sewing skills and young men in computer knowledge so they can be employed to earn a living. Similarly the village people she has helped produce Khmer handicrafts have been nurtured in the faith and many are now attending a small church and growing spiritually.

There are still areas that need de-mining and every month there are currently 60 to 90 new landmine victims. The de-miners are clearing 300 metres each side of the road so the road access is safe but beyond that, the fields are still full of mines. Hungry people are moving about and trying to find new land to grow vegetables and plant rice to survive, but when they have built their little thatch houses many die or are maimed for life by hitting a landmine in their own back garden. The Halo Trust from England has a thousand workers and the Cambodia Mines Advisory Group is working continuously, but it will be years before these merciless mines are totally cleared.

Some of the amputees were soldiers in the Cambodian forces and many are double amputees. It is still a massive task and these victims do not want to beg as they feel ashamed and unwanted. To help in this area, Marie has joined with a local NGO who make wooden carts for these amputees to sit in and sell books or handicrafts to the tourists. She has a small Bible study group for amputees and is linking them into the local church. The children of the amputees are now attending a Sunday school, and they really enjoy having crayons to draw pictures and learn about the love of Jesus. Even some of these little children are amputees, as they have wandered into wooded areas to play and have struck a hidden landmine. Marie finds it a delight to teach these children the Christian message because they are so open to the faith and listen with great attention to the stories from the Bible. She also teaches them praise songs and being musically minded, they love singing praises to their Jesus. Some of these children go out begging for their families because they have nothing to eat, so their Sundays are special days when they can be children again and not go on the streets begging to support the family.

Marie attends a church which was established by a Khmer pastor called Sarai. In the past he was a soldier and committed some small offence whereby he had a month's prison sentence. In jail he drew a keyboard on the wall of his cell and learnt from written music how to play the instrument. He led the worship in a church in Siem Reap but then felt he should leave to go back to Phnom Penh and live in community along with a man from Hosanna Ministries. In this community they refuse any money offers from outside but all work to make a living and live together in harmony.

This church in Siem Reap is now led by a lay pastor who does not receive any payment. He works in a Korean business and everyone else has a job so they are concentrating on learning the deeper lessons of the faith in order to grow before they go out to evangelise. There are several other churches in Siem Reap that are growing well. This area that was once the centre of ancient Khmer Buddhist culture, bound up with the worship of idols, now has many gatherings of believers who praise the great eternal God for saving them.

Another church leader who has an amazing story, in common with the other jewels of Cambodia, is Pastor Navvy from Sisophon, a town over one hundred kilometres from Siem Reap on the road to Thailand halfway to the border.

Pastor Navvy

Having met each other in the refugee camp when Marie first began her ministry to refugees, she had been impressed with Pastor Navvy's honesty and integrity. He lives in a northern town where there is quite a big industry in gem mining. Jewels in Cambodia are very varied both in beauty, colour and value, but unfortunately there were unscrupulous gem merchants in the Pol Pot era who exchanged these jewels for weapons of war and landmines.

Pastor Navvy's church is relatively small with a congregation of about 40. He studied at New Life Bible School in Phnom Penh. Marie arranged for him to meet me at her flat while I was in Siem Reap.

Navvy was in Cambodia through the Pol Pot years and had great difficulties and hardship, but he found the Vietnamese occupation equally bad. They sent a large number of Khmers to work in an area that was known for its malaria and landmines forcing them to labour from dawn to dusk with little food to eat. Being brought up a Buddhist he had never heard about the Christian faith, neither did he want to learn about it. Eventually the conditions he was in were so bad that 28 of them banded together and decided to escape to the nearest refugee camp on the Thai border. The Vietnamese soldiers tried to capture them but they persevered until they reached a point of total exhaustion and starvation.

Pastor Navvy with his family

Ten of the original number were killed by landmines and the rest continued the desperate bid for freedom in a state of extreme weakness, until their numbers fell to five: the others died of starvation and disease. In a state of total despair the remaining five lay down to wait for death and gave up all hope of ever being able to reach the refugee camp. Navvy looked up to the sky and said in a weak whisper, 'God who made me, help me.' He had no knowledge of God at that point in his life but to his amazement he heard a voice that said, 'Stand up and you will live.' Startled by this voice, he asked the four remaining companions if they had heard it. None of them had but as he stood up the rest of his friends did the same and, trying to walk in their weak state, they saw a banana tree in front of them so they all ate some bananas and, strengthened by this food, they reached Site Two camp in 1986.

In the camp, Navvy heard Christians telling their message but he had no intention of getting involved with them because his family were very staunch Buddhists and for him to change faith would be a disgrace. One of his friends gave him a Bible to read and only because there was nothing else to do, he began to read it. As he read the Bible through from Genesis to Revelation, it made him think more about God. The creation story really caught his attention and he started to think it must have been this Creator God who had spoken to him. He heard the gospel in the camp but resented those evangelising Christians. Finally he was so impressed with the story of creation, that he agreed to go to camp meetings that were held in an orphanage and he listened to a little group of Kampuchean Krom believers. This was organised by Campus Crusade for Christ. He continued to read the Bible daily and on his third reading of the whole Bible he got the message that Jesus, his Redeemer, was in the beginning with God.

He made a commitment to Christ but it didn't last long. Giving his Bible away to friends who were not believers, they used the paper to make cigarettes. He still left God out of his life and began to suffer from severe headaches. He was convinced that these were caused by evil spirits tormenting him because he had left his family traditions; he remembered being taught that the spirits of the dead can attack anyone who goes away from ancestor worship.

At the end of the year he became ill with a really vicious strain of malaria and was admitted to hospital as his life was ebbing away. Some people from YWAM came to minister to him but he was too ill to take much in. The camp doctor visited him and told him he would die. He asked the doctor to take his bones back to Cambodia but when the doctor left he suddenly thought – this has happened to me because I left God out of my life! He prayed in great weakness, said he was sorry and asked God to make him well again. As he prayed he felt the fever lifting from his body and in three days he was well. Immediately, he made a promise to God, 'Because you have saved my life I will be your servant forever.' He was moved to the camp where Marie was working with the children and teaching them to make handicrafts. She drew alongside Navvy and taught him more about the faith, so that he was able to become a lay pastor of the little church Marie had established in the camp.

Returning to Cambodia in 1993 with other Christian converts from the camp, he set up a small group in his home town of Sisophon. He went to Phnom Penh for two years to train at the New Life Bible School then returned to pastor the church in Sisophon. He married in 1996 and now has a son and one adopted daughter who was an unwanted orphan. He purchased a plot of land next to the local government official's house and began to build a church; then he faced serious threats from this local official who wanted the land for his own purposes. Finally the official told him that he would have a gun at his head if he did not give him the land. Local officials could carry out a threat like this as often the new legislation laid down by the central government is not practised in areas far from the city.

The opposition he was under was so intense that he made the journey to Phnom Penh and was able to speak with the prime minister. He came away with papers stating clearly that the land was church property. The church has grown but there are problems with missions who go to Sisophon, and other places, with well-intentioned but unhelpful schemes offering free rice and other commodities.

This has caused division in his church. Navvy recognises that both approaches can represent Christianity though the methods of inducement used by some missions can be disconcerting at times.

While ministering in a quiet village nearby, he was called to see a man whose wife had been shot dead by robbers. He built up a relationship with this man and comforted him in his bereavement. Later this widower expressed an interest in the Christian faith so Navvy continued to meet with him and eventually told him the whole gospel message. When Navvy described the two eternal destinations, heaven and hell, the man was terrified and made a commitment to follow Jesus. Navvy missed him for a while and was told by neighbours that he had been arrested on charges of mass genocide. It was only when he was arrested that Navvy knew his name. This unknown man was actually the infamous Deuch who is still in prison awaiting trial. Others also had some impact on Deuch's life but his conversion is real (see chapter eight). It is still uncertain when he and Ta Mok (who was once deputy to Pol Pot) will ever face trial, even though they have both been held under arrest in Phnom Penh for some years.

CHAPTER FIFTEEN:

A Hidden Jewel:
Phen Dararith

Marie talked of the lack of books or teaching cassette tapes presenting a problem in the churches for new converts to grow in the faith. Radio plays a significant part, but there are plenty of good Khmer writers and books on all subjects were needed. In renewing links with Steve Westergren who had followed his father in being a leader in the Christian and Missionary Alliance (CAMA), I discovered a shared vision for a publishing house. He told me the church had grown at the fastest rate in its history from 1993 to 1997. The rate of growth started to slow a little in 1997, not because of the coup and general instability but because it was very much a fledgling church that needed to strengthen its wings to fly higher. His concern now was to see the church put down good roots into Bible teaching and discipleship. The area of greatest need was in good literature and Bible study books. His father had printed the first Bible which was translated by Revd Hammond and produced in New York. Government permission was granted for its distribution in 1953. Having considered the idea of a publishing house for years, 90 per cent of the funds were now in place and he hoped to start the publishing house very soon.

Asking him how he saw the church today he said it was exciting to be a part of this growing church but there was a need for the new converts to really learn what it meant to live a life in Christ. The young church needed solid teaching in biblical principles of daily living. The radio broadcasts were a good resource but the need for books was greater. Daily Bible reading resources needed to be written by Khmer writers with culturally appropriate illustrations.

The EFC plays a significant role in helping people to work together, and CAMA is a member. It had 15 churches under its umbrella to begin with but there are now 101, so the body of Christ in Cambodia is definitely growing under its direction but a discipleship strategy is needed to address problems of lack of depth.

There are now two translations of the Bible and the Bible Society has played a helpful role in a new translation. The old and new both complement each other so both are good. Steve plans to publish a basic resource called *Look, Learn and Listen*, with pictures but only 50 per cent of the church will benefit as the rest are illiterate. Education is a major problem because the government often does not pay its teachers so the quality is poor or non-existent. At first Steve will publish these basic resources, then a Bible commentary.

His overall view of the church growth is interesting. There has been a large influx of missions, both good and bad but as some benefit what does it matter? The greatest church planter of all time had the same trouble in Philippians 1:15–18: 'It is true that some preach Christ out of envy and rivalry, but others out of good will. The latter do so in love, knowing that I am put here for the defence of the gospel. The former preach Christ out of selfish ambition, not sincerely, supposing that they can stir up trouble for me while I am in chains. But what does it matter? The important thing is that in every way, whether from false motives or true, Christ is preached. And because of this I rejoice.' God has chosen people from all sorts of backgrounds to help rebuild the church; there are people from Taiwan, Singapore, Malaysia, South Korea and the Philippines to count a few. All have different methods but God has used some unlikely sources too.

We know about the bad influence that UNTAC brought with them but the good needs to be told. Of the 22,000 soldiers that came to the country, 4,000 of them were Christians. They were sent throughout the country but before they were dispatched many of them came to CAMA and asked for tracts and Scripture portions in Khmer to distribute to these outlying places. When the refugees came back from the camps and had learnt about Christ they returned to their towns and villages to find small groups of interested believers who had read these tracts. They were followed up by missionaries, but also a significant number were helped to establish churches by Barnabas' ministries.

The government has had a positive role, sometimes in being too busy fighting each other to be bothered with such a small minority of Christians, but now the influence of the leading Khmers such as Revd Heng Cheng plays a very important role. Looking back on his history in Cambodia, he says in 1991 he was in a very small group in Phnom Penh who met for prayer for the country. It was dark spiritually and physically in every way. There were frequent power cuts and a lot of violence. In that little group they focused on God's promises for this land. One of those members had a promise they felt was from God. It was that in God's timing this beleaguered land would one day become the Lighthouse for the region.

God has done great things for this church, beginning as it did in the refugee camps where distressed and wounded people heard of a God of love and compassion. In a strange way the Khmer Rouge were used to scatter Cambodians throughout the world, not just to the refugee camps. Returnees have been signally used of God to build the church; others who took resettlement in western countries have helped to build Cambodian churches there. The current president of EFC, Pastor Pon Sokha spent several years in the States and had a ministry there, but on his return to Cambodia he has been a great influence in helping with the unity of churches. Having lived in America, he can see why opposition arises over some missions, and is able to help.

Phen Dararith

One incredible contributor – whose life's work was done in obscurity and severe ill health – will be blessing the new church long after being called to his eternal home. Phen Dararith had been a university student in Phnom Penh during the sixties. After graduation he moved to California. He died aged sixty in August 2003, when Steve had this clear vision to pioneer a publishing house in Phnom Penh with Khmer writers. Someone told Steve about this man who had died. Going to his hometown, Steve discovered that he had suffered from colon cancer for many years, having survived a colostomy, but lived in poor health on welfare money. His wife worked hard to find the extra money that enabled them to make ends meet. Throughout his illness Dararith worked on a Bible commentary, an outline on the epistle to the Ephesians and a Bible dictionary too! All those years ago he had been a youth leader in a church in Phnom Penh. It was only after his death that this valuable resource came to light and these books will be the first items that Steve hopes to publish.

Since this discovery Steve has met a number of people who were impacted by this sick man. His life has passed away but this is an example of how God set his heart on this nation 80 years ago. Times of extremity woke up the nation and scattered it. The part we each play is just a facet of the whole picture. God is the Master Artist who knows the finished canvas, and it will be the most beautiful work of art that only the great Creator God could produce. Some hidden jewels will come to light, and receive their reward.

Chhirc Taing was a product of CAMA ministries in Cambodia and Steve's father played his part in helping to establish him in the faith. It was Chhirc Taing who motivated English Christians to begin SAO Cambodia: Barnabas sat under the ministry of Cliff Westergren in the camps; Revd Heng Cheng made a commitment to Christ through a CAMA pastor in Vietnam. These lives are the result of the faithfulness of others, many of whom are now in their eternal homes. Finally Steve said, 'Take this message to England: "You can have an impact if you are faithful."'

CHAPTER SIXTEEN:

Faith in Action through World Vision

Further insight into church growth in Cambodia can be seen in the work of World Vision. Despite their Memorandum of Understanding with the government that they concentrate on development projects, I heard many reports of Cambodians coming to know the Lord through World Vision. The government agreement does not prohibit individuals speaking of their faith to their friends or colleagues nor helping to nurture them into discipleship.

Brian Maher works for the Christian Impact Programme of World Vision, which begins with spiritual nurturing of staff, holistic Christian witness of members and working on church relations. The beauty of this approach is that churches happen through World Vision. Every member of staff is given the knowledge of the Christian faith and left to make a decision to follow Christ. No one is forced to do this but if they do decide to follow the pathway of faith, they are helped to integrate into a suitable church.

An annual retreat day is held for staff and over the last six years they have seen about one hundred Buddhists become Christians. They have seen churches spring up out of their development projects but they do not proselytise. Brian affirmed:

People ask us, why do you risk your life through landmines, bandits, storms, through the Khmer Rouge and then you look after us when your day has finished? Why are you not more concerned to be at home and enjoy your life with your own people? 1 Peter 3:15 says, 'Always be prepared to give an answer … [to the hope that is within you],' and that is what we expect our Christian staff to do. When they tell people that the love of Jesus motivates them, they ask questions as to this Jesus and often they become Christians through these discussions.

A church that grew out of this witnessing is in Kompong Thom, a central province of Cambodia. World Vision staff went to this area despite the fact that the Khmer Rouge was operating as bandits and there were hundreds of landmines that still needed to be cleared. They began development work in a village where there was a man who was a wife-beater, drunkard, a gambler who borrowed money and never returned it. His conduct was so bad that the villagers kicked him out of the place. He came back to visit his family and saw a group of World Vision people and he said, 'Who are these people, why are they training locals to work, they have credit lending, rice banks and cow banks, why do they do this?' He began attending the Village Development Committee meetings and was astonished at the big improvements in village life. The meetings always began with prayer, so he was even more intrigued to find out what god they spoke to.

Other development meetings took place in the next town so he attended them as well and was amazed at the Bible readings and prayer times. When he began to ask questions about the faith the staff spent all the time they could to tell him about Jesus. He said he wanted to become a Christian and changed his behaviour dramatically, so much so that the village agreed to have him back. He told all the villagers about Christ and they began a Bible study. This eventually led to a small church in the village. This man grew in the faith, received teaching in the word and became their pastor. The church grew rapidly under the ministry of Pastor Kuen and he now leads outreaches to other villages.

World Vision employ 700 staff in Cambodia, two-thirds are Christian; the rest are Buddhist. They have a very comprehensive view in strong Christian teachings to the staff so they became aware of the need for their conduct to be in keeping with biblical standards. The Cambodian church is a young church and does not always have the concept of everything coming into line with biblical teaching. Often, converted World Vision staff who are employed in the village setting are so well taught through their daily devotions that they end up being in leadership in their local churches and some go on to become pastors.

FEBC transmits Christian programmes and in one area where there has never been a missionary or any Christian influence, there were people who listened to these broadcasts and wanted to be Christians. They met together just to hear the radio programmes, but had no idea of how to start a church. World Vision went to this area and found this group meeting together, not knowing what else to do; so they helped them to form a little church and supplied them with Bibles and Christian leaflets, then taught them how to conduct a church service. With such a small beginning, that group has grown and is now being discipled by a trained pastor.

Brian is a co-director along with Uon Seila of the Youth Commission of EFC so his input to the younger generation has had a very good response. I attended a church that had been structured to meet the younger generation for Christ and so change some of the bad aspects of society. In the west we are unaware of some of these problems but the appalling rise in AIDS is an example of this.

Suan Both with his family

Suan Both

Suan is a Cambodian man who had been employed by World Vision when he and his family were not Christians. Both he and his wife spoke immaculate English and had a gentle sincere character. After the Pol Pot years Suan joined the Military School and was totally immersed in his career, having joined the Khmer Peoples Liberation Forces to fight against the Vietnamese occupation. In the course of his career he went to Malaysia, and his wife who was left in Cambodia was forced to go to Khao I Dang refugee camp as she and her children were starving.

Suan returned to Cambodia to discover that his wife had gone to the camp. He was dreadfully upset and made a decision to leave the army immediately and go straight to the camp to find her. He was reunited with his wife and family but was refused refugee status and classified as an illegal immigrant. Aware of these problems he just kept a very low profile and remained hidden from the authorities.

While in the camp he heard the Christian message from Seventh Day Adventists and Catholics but was not interested as he thought all religions were the same and he was not interested in any of them. When he was sent back to Phnom Penh for the elections in 1993 he had no home and no income. After five months of living precariously and in great need, he applied for a post with World Vision and was appointed as Project Manager in Kompong Thom Province.

The daily devotions of the staff sparked off a real interest in his heart to learn more about Christianity. He was given a Bible and as he asked for help they arranged for him to take part in Bible studies. The turning point in his life was when Barnabas arrived and preached the gospel. With deep emotion Suan told me he repented deeply over his life and made a strong commitment to follow Jesus. 'It was the loving, compassionate character of Barnabas, who showed such real concern for my soul that made me repent,' he said.

World Vision introduced him to a local church led by an old man, Ngov Van who had remained at his post faithfully through all the hard years, caring for his little flock. Suan was baptised at this church which has about 70 members, and he grew in the faith because the pastor had some good teaching books in English. He shared his faith with many others and began to teach them Christian values from the English books. The old pastor is still there but he is training younger men as he is now partially sighted.

While Suan and his family grew in that church another man in the village was converted from a background of witchcraft. Later the grace of God spoke to his family and they accepted Christ. Finally, the elderly mother, who was the ruling witch in the village, was thoroughly converted and burnt all her witchcraft symbols. News of this conversion brought many more to the church.

Through the Village Community Development people learn about Christ step by step. World Vision staff arrange community seminars for interested believers and through this approach they grow in the faith. In Kompong Chhnang, a project supported by the UK assists the local people in growing vegetables, raising pigs and chickens, and teaching handicraft skills, on a revolving loan scheme. They are all taught to work together and learn to love each other. World Vision arranges Family Retreats where they help to sort out marital problems with believers who have an unbelieving partner. Suan Both, with his wife and children, told me that becoming Christians has totally changed their lives and they never forget the love and compassion that they received from Barnabas. God has also used Nigel Goddard, who has helped to train Suan Both in management skills, to strengthen his faith.

CHAPTER SEVENTEEN:

Diamonds in the Dark:
Aid for AIDS

In addition to the Language School, Agnes Verner has links with a number of different outreaches: caring for street kids, hosting young people from the New Life Church, teaching Bible studies, visiting hospitals, running the Mercy Home. One such work is a church in operation reaching out to people under the sentence of death from AIDS in the Military Hospital.

Marie Ens had started this work and returned to Cambodia from Canada after her husband Norman had been taken to be with the Lord. Norman and Marie Ens first went to Cambodia in 1961 as church planters with CAMA. Marie returned in 1994 to help the pastor of the New Jerusalem Church who had initiated the 'church in the hospital'. To begin with, she found the work daunting but soon other members from the churches caught the vision of these dying souls and today there are in the region of 30 helpers coming on a regular basis. Otherwise, when a member of the military becomes ill with AIDS they are admitted to the hospital but the family of the patient has to provide the food and care for his needs. Many have no relatives in a position to help them.

I had visited several hospitals in Phnom Penh but the AIDS section of the Military Hospital shocked me. I commented on the conditions to Agnes but she assured me that it had all improved considerably since they received help from the church. The grounds near the AIDS unit had refuse with chickens scrapping about for food. Some women were cooking food over little wood fires.

We visited a young man who was still wearing his military uniform, probably because he had no other clothes. He was in a small dark room with his pretty wife, two children and mother-in-law. Many Cambodian hospitals do not supply food for the patients so if they have relatives, they sometimes partially move into the hospital room to cater for the patient. But when the wife and children move in, they are often HIV positive as well. The 30 or more Cambodian Christians with Marie went round the wards with fresh fruit and other little essentials like soap and sweets for the children. They build up a friendship with the patients showing love and care to them and then begin telling them of a Saviour God who can give them eternal life. They said the patients are open to hearing the good news so they make sure they really understand what salvation means. As the time comes when they know they will die they are so sweet and trusting in the Lord. Marie said, 'This is a very motivating work, once you start you can't stop because it is so rewarding to see these sick and dying people find peace and a certainty that they will go to heaven when they die.'

Observing the Christians from the New Jerusalem Church speaking so lovingly to the dying patients in this bleak hospital, it seemed such an appropriate name. Those redeemed by the blood of Jesus through hearing the message of forgiveness through the ministry of this church, will one day be in the Holy City, the new Jerusalem, where there will be neither sickness nor death. These patients are moving from the land of the dying into the land of the living because they have had a personal encounter with the

Light of the World. Another positive aspect of this unusual church is that they are ministering to the wives who are pregnant, and organise a caring nurse to give neviripine, an anti-retroviral drug to the wives before they go into labour. A dose of this drug is given to the new-born child and 70 per cent of the children are not HIV positive. Sometimes the mother's life is also spared. This has to be monitored far more than they would like because all the sick patients have been living on their wits with no money. They will sell on a drug to make enough money to gamble; but a worse scenario is that the doctors are so corrupt they take the drug from the patient and sell it on for their own gain, and substitute it with a worthless tablet.

We left the hospital and travelled outside the city to a country area where Marie lives in a house in a compound of an orphanage and a community centre for people with AIDS. Colourful gardens surround the 16 neat wood-and-thatch houses, with a workshop for sewing nearby. A lady is employed to teach sewing to the mothers and keep them occupied for as long as they are able. The school has a well-equipped playground which Samaritan's Purse had funded. The whole complex has been built with a plan to make life as comfortable as possible. Part of the ministry of this caring lady was to help the mothers who were dying from AIDS who come to the orphanage with their children. When the mother dies, the children then have some security in being able to stay in the same place.

One lady living there was called Lin. She was only in her mid-thirties; her once glossy black hair had fallen out, she had sores all over her body and was going blind. Marie confirmed she had only a little time to live. Her eleven-year-old daughter, Ny, was attending the school. The dying lady's story was one that could be told over and over again. Her husband had died of AIDS long ago; left destitute she lived rough under a market stall with just a mosquito net for a covering. Her daughter was sent out to beg, so they both lived on their wits, stealing, begging; and the mother, when she could find any money, drank alcohol to ease the pain of her existence. As I looked into her partially sighted eyes and listened to her moans of suffering, my heart ached for these people who had such a terrible existence. But what would have happened if there were no caring Christians to take her in and care for her needs when she died? Marie had told her gently of the love of Jesus and how believing in him, all the sins of her past failures were washed away and she would go to be with him when she died. The love and compassion of Jesus had been ministered to this tragic, sick and dying lady. How much do we care for these souls that are of infinite value to our wonderful caring heavenly Father?

Two months later Lin died and Ny attended the cremation. Now she was an orphan but she would be safe in the care of the orphanage. However, only three months after Lin's death, an older son arrived at the orphanage on a motorbike with a much older woman. Giving some money to the watching children, he told them not to say anything to the carers. Calling Ny, he told her to get on the motorbike and rode off. The children went to the manager who had a car; he immediately drove out of the orphanage to catch up with the motorbike. Thankfully he soon came alongside the bike and shouted to the brother, 'Stop or I'll call the police! Ny, get in the car.' She did as she was told and the brother was ordered not to return to the orphanage without permission, and if he did the police would be told. His intention had been to sell his little sister for $500 to the brothel owner.

Another young wife with five children had AIDS and three of her children were also infected. She held in her arms a little eighteen-month-old boy who was very sick. Marie told me he had AIDS and tuberculosis. In the bright sunshine, with the peaceful rice paddies, dark green sugar palms nearby in all their beauty, it seemed so sad that here were people in the prime of life facing a premature death through this terrible disease. The children who survive are given the anti-retroviral drug and there is a full-time doctor who genuinely cares, who does all he can to ease the pain of those dying from the disease.

There were older children who were in their late teens. One of them helped in the school to teach the younger children. It was such a haven of rest and beauty contrasting with the dark, depressing hospital and it was supported by Christians that Marie had motivated to give financially when she returned to speak about her work in Canada and elsewhere. A large well-kept community centre for widows and their children was nearby with vegetable gardens, and chicken and pig rearing – with a dual motive of teaching them how to raise these farm animals to meet their own needs – and a school with a playground.

Marie and Agnes visit the dying in the Military Hospital faithfully every week, bringing the only hope that there is for them; that of eternal life through knowing the Man of Sorrows. He sees their darkness and their suffering, and he will gather the little ones as a shepherd carries the lambs that are sick. He will carry them away to the place that has no more sorrow and pain. This ministry is costly work, but when I think of Marie, Agnes and those from the New Jerusalem Church bringing light into such darkness, they are diamonds that shine in the dark with the love of Christ. Diamonds are formed from carbon under heat, pressure and time. Carbon is a totally black substance, yet under pressure, with heat and time it can become the most precious of all jewels – a diamond. When diamonds are found they need cutting and polishing before they sparkle. Refining processes are often painful but they produce the finest jewels.

In the west, many think that if people get AIDS it's their own fault. However, to help with understanding the problems of Cambodia, it seems appropriate to retell a shocking but true story that Marie tells in her inspiring book, *A Time for Mercy* (Pennsylvania: Christian Publications Inc., 1998):

> Some children in Cambodia are forced to live a nightmarish existence. The exploitation of these young innocents prompted me to compose the following plea for prayer. God who hears prayer will surely answer the cries of his daughters in many lands on behalf of their sisters in Cambodia.
>
> Tears filled Rames' dark eyes as she blurted out the news, 'My daughter is missing. She went out to find a job and she never came home. We have looked everywhere and don't know where to find her.' Her listeners received the news in shocked silence. With sickening certainty they knew where this lovely teenager had been taken. Unquestionably her sweet innocent face and lovely young body had already brought evil delight to some despicable man who would pay $500 for undamaged merchandise.
>
> As the days dragged into weeks, the mother and her friends pleaded with God to rescue His little one who had put her trust in Him. Finally, after a full month the answer came. 'Give me $10,' offered the vile woman 'and I will show you the house where I left her.' 'Give us $100,' demanded the loathsome brothel owners, 'and you can have her back.' In response to the mother's pitiful pleadings, the price was reduced to $70. What joy filled the mother's heart to be reunited with her daughter! But

what revulsion and agony to discover she had been abused ten times a night! And so she came home, confused, sick in body and damaged in spirit, her most priceless treasure stolen forever away. The healing process would begin as she was assured of the love of her family, her friends and especially her Saviour.

The mother, driven by fury and a deep desire to protect other youngsters reported the crime to the authorities. She told her sad story. Her daughter had to suffer the indignity of countless embarrassing questions. The wicked brothel owners were called in for questioning. And the result:- the mother was rewarded a paltry $100 – so much for the world's justice!

And so we are introduced to this dark, filthy, stinking swamp of degradation in Cambodian society: the prostitution of children. We want to turn away. Our minds loathe dwelling on the depravity that would cause a woman to trick a teenager into entering a brothel with the promise of a legitimate job. We cannot fathom the depths of iniquity that would permit a mother to sell her own daughter to be abused for the rest of her life. We recoil from the thought of young boys becoming the sad toys of despicable men. But, we must look, we must know and we must care. Where can a child go? If not to the parents, if not to the governing authorities, if not to society, where can a child go to find protection and justice? Who will say to this monstrous evil, 'Stop!'?

We will say it! We women who know how to pray will unite our hearts in a mighty cry to the great Judge who rules over all! We will petition Him to cause strong laws to be established and enforced that will hinder people like the vile brothel owners. We will plead with God to move by His mighty Spirit causing poverty stricken mothers to treasure their daughters above silver or gold, willing rather to die of starvation than to sell them. We will beg Him to protect young boys and girls from being lied to by predators. We will fight the enemy of the souls of Cambodian children by our prayers

As I close this dark chapter, can I plead with my readers, pray, give and support the needs of this gentle land that is still suffering from the pagan past, terrible wars, dire poverty, injustices: and the lack of care from those of us who live in comfort in the west? The New Jerusalem Church, touched by the love and compassion of Christ, empowered by his Spirit and motivated by hearts filled with gratitude for his great love to them, is one of the jewels shining in the darkest places of Cambodia. Only when those devoted souls reach the final new Jerusalem will they find the rewards that he has in place for them eternally.

CHAPTER EIGHTEEN:

A New Generation:
the Youth Commission

The EFC is well aware of the need to instruct and prepare the hearts of the next generation in Cambodia so this scourge of AIDS is under control. Brian Maher (co-director with Seila of the Youth Commission of the EFC) visited Cambodia in 1990 and 1992 when he caught a vision to help the youth of Cambodia and moved his family to Phnom Penh in 1994. Brian has a most interesting history that led him to Cambodia in that year. He worked as a forester for five years in the States and then went on to a small Bible institute in Schroon Lake, New York, where he met a group of Cambodian Christian youth who came up from Bridgeport, Connecticut for winter camp. Most could not speak English very well and had come from the Khao I Dang refugee camp a few years earlier. Since he was an older student, he was in charge of this group of 50 Cambodian teenagers for a full week. He had such an interesting experience working with them that he prayed he might someday help these people in their own country. Their recent history had been full of tragedy, the effects of Pol Pot and the Khmer Rouge, could not be erased overnight: it would take generations to work out. Brian's heart was set on helping these young people and through this encounter he was called to Cambodia.

In the late 1980s, Brian was Youth Minister at Calvary Baptist Church, Darien, and married with two children. Then he was able to raise support for them all to go to Cambodia with 'Mission to Unreached Peoples' in 1994. Currently he is working with World Vision Cambodia as an advisor to their Christian Impact department – as we read in chapter sixteen – and he has helped to establish a centre for training young Khmer Christians into leadership roles under the umbrella of EFC. HIV/AIDS is decimating Cambodia, and a large part of the programme deals with sexual awareness and prevention of HIV/AIDS and other related STDs, from a biblical perspective. Another main thrust of youth work is to help Cambodian Christian youth to take part and have a voice in the rebuilding of Cambodia, rather than being passive Christians.

The EFC Youth Commission organises an annual youth conference at Sihanoukville – on the coast. These events have been successful bringing together campers, organisers, teachers and speakers from Mennonites, Campus Crusade for Christ, AOG, Baptists, Methodists (and so the list goes on) to reach the new generation for Christ and teach them godly standards for living. Barnabas and Revd Heng Cheng and other leaders from EFC give the keynote addresses. Revd Pon Sokha, the president, led a great camp-fire service on one of these occasions urging youth to find their motivation to serve God in the knowledge of God himself, rather than in external factors, like using service for getting a job. He said many had mixed motives and he called them to a fresh commitment to serve out of joy for the Lord rather than for personal benefit.

The EFC Youth Commission was born largely through the vision of Revd Pon Sokha. He has a vision to see Cambodian youth disciplined, trained and mobilised as a force that can stem the decay in Khmer society and be salt and light within contemporary culture. Revd Pon Sokha escaped Cambodia to the Thai border camps in 1980 and was resettled in the States where he led a Cambodian church before moving back to Cambodia with his family in 1992.

Brian met Revd Sokha while he was studying at the King's College in Briarcliff Manor, New York, and shared some stories about his experiences in Cambodia as well as some of the unique experiences that confronted his people when they first entered the United States as refugees. Sokha's Cambodian church was a large one and consisted of refugees from the Killing Fields era. He cared deeply about each member of his flock and visited others who he wanted to help settle into such a strange new land. These refugees needed a lot of care as they settled into such an alien culture. Sokha made regular visits to his flock to see how they were getting on.

One visiting day Sokha had to travel at a time when the highway was very quiet. Driving along, he saw an object in the middle of the highway. As he got closer, he noticed it was a rather large snapping turtle. Being away from his native Cambodia, he missed having a delicious bowl of turtle soup every now and then. So he slowed down and pulled his car off the highway onto the grass. He opened the hatchback of his Nissan and went to snatch the turtle which weighed close to 70 pounds. Sokha cautiously lifted it up and carefully carried it to the back of his car, where there was space for a turtle to be comfortable.

Cruising down route 91 Sokha had other things on his mind. He had forgotten about the turtle until he heard some rustling under his seat. The turtle had moved and was wedged under the driver's seat of his car. As he looked down, the turtle's head was sticking out between his legs. He pulled over on the six-lane highway and tried to move the turtle. But in spite of tools and all sorts of devices his attempts to dislodge the turtle were useless. He had to drive on but God was gracious; Sokha soon came upon a service station and pulled in. Americans are not too patient when it comes to serving foreigners so the mechanic, clenching a short stub of cigar between his teeth muttered, 'Whaddya want, bub?' Sokha replied, 'Sir, I have a problem, I need your help. I have a large turtle stuck under the driver's seat of my car.' 'What! Lemme have a look at dis.' The incredulous mechanic thought he had seen everything but this seemed to top it all.

Sokha suggested that the mechanic remove the seat but the man said, 'Sure, just gimme two minutes to call Channel Eight news.' Sokha pleaded with the man not to call the TV station but he went ahead. God once again came to Sokha's rescue. The TV crew was tied up elsewhere. The amused mechanic amicably removed the car seat and a local pick-up truck offered to take the grand-daddy of snapping turtles back to the nearest pond.

Another time, Sokha decided to visit an older member of his flock whom he thought could do with some help. It took him a long while to find the house and when he did, there didn't appear to be a doorbell. So he entered a screened-in porch and saw loads of boxes of empty tins of cat food. 'Boy,' Sokha said to himself, 'this man must have a lot of cats.' He stowed away this titbit of information perhaps to use as small talk later.

Recognising Sokha and happy to see him, the man invited him in. After a while Sokha had still not seen a single cat. He waited another half an hour and still not a single peep, meow or tail poking from behind a piece of furniture. At this point Sokha's curiosity got the better of him.

'Uncle, where do you keep your cats?'

'Cats?' the man replied, 'I hate cats. What makes you think I have a cat, let alone cats?'

Sokha said, 'Well, Uncle, when I was waiting for you to open the door I noticed all those boxes of empty cat food tins.'

'Cat food?' said the older Cambodian man. 'Those are cans of fish I bought at the supermarket.'

Sokha realised that the man must have been eating cat food with his rice for years, so said, 'Why didn't you tell me you had no money? We could have helped you rather than resort to eating cat food.'

Uncle replied, 'I can't read English but I can recognise the prices on the cans. I just bought what I thought was the lowest price tuna.'

The Maher family arrived in Cambodia in August 1994. They stayed with Revd Sokha and his wife for two weeks, getting to know them and learning to love them most of all. Not long after Brian began to assist Sokha at the office of Cambodia Christian Services. Over those next two years, the EFC was to replace Cambodian Christian Services and both Brian and Sokha moved over to the EFC. Sokha served as the first general secretary while Brian began to facilitate the birth of Cambodia's first Christian Youth movement. This movement has had a significant place in helping to establish a new generation in the faith.

During my 2003 visit I attended a New Life Fellowship in Phnom Penh, led by Pastor Chuck McCaul and his wife, Cynde. It was a lively, well-attended group where there were large numbers of young people. Chuck is training young Cambodians to assist in church planting and pastoral work. New Life Foundation, the relief and developmental organisation (linked with the church) which the McCauls direct in Cambodia, has a number of projects including orphanages, community health care and an Office Skills Training School where young people learn English, typing, basic computer skills and other office-related subjects for no fee. Successful candidates are then helped to find jobs.

Agnes Verner taught a Bible study group at this fellowship and the early morning prayer meetings were well attended by the young people who prayed and interceded for a new generation to set standards in Cambodia for a holy lifestyle in Christian commitment. Agnes hosted evenings in her home where the same young people made pancakes and had a time of fellowship together. The generation of new converts in Cambodia really make a serious commitment to pray.

Brian Maher has joined the board of EFC with the purpose of enlarging their youth work. At a recent meeting he observed the larger part of the board consisted of Cambodian church leaders, both young and old. But expatriates were also present, consisting of two Americans, Steve Westergren and himself. Attending this meeting was a foreign lady with a few other Cambodians. Brian said:

> During the meeting I looked around the room at the Cambodians. I knew of the hurts they had received at the hands of foreign missionaries. I understood the cultural dynamics between the three levels of Cambodian leaders: a) those that had an uninterrupted education and received their high school diploma before 1975, b) those that had never got past the eighth grade and c) those now coming up through the ranks of weak secondary school education, some with Bible school training. I also knew the tensions between Cambodian pastors resettled overseas from the border camps in the early eighties and who returned in the nineties with theological qualifications. Lastly I was aware of the issues between those who were trapped in the camps for many years and those who considered themselves true patriots for remaining behind in Cambodia.

Another thing that I noticed was the foreign woman on the board and a Cambodian woman facilitating the meeting. The level of dynamics in that room was enough to keep a truck load of sociologists going for years. I want you to know that I was witnessing a real miracle. Not too many years ago, such meetings as this would not have had a woman present. Cambodian pastors now talk about wisdom, patience, forgiveness and how not to rejoice much in successes but rather in the fact that our Father in heaven loves us.

Brian asks for prayer for the EFC as it goes into a new future for the Cambodian church. But who was the foreign woman who has just recently joined the board of the EFC?

CHAPTER NINETEEN:

Far above Rubies:
Milet's vision

Milet Goddard was no foreigner to me! I was able to reassure Brian that EFC had acquired one of the jewels of Cambodia! She is assisting the general secretary of EFC and helping to build up its administrative capacity to service the growing church. Before that she worked with FAITH (Food And Income, Training and Health) a project of ICC working in partnership with EFC. The Khmer advisors working for FAITH help local 'core groups' of Christians to motivate village people to help themselves. This work has also brought about spiritual results and there is a new local church that will be self-supporting in the near future.

One experience I had of the project work was to attend a training session at the New Jerusalem Church for FAITH project workers. These meetings are held periodically and lay leaders, with Christians from the provinces, come to learn from one another. The praises from the group could be heard in the road and it was a wonderful sound, spreading the good news to the neighbourhood. The pastor of this church is Revd Bin David. He is a musician and composer who became a Christian through the ministry of CAMA.

This is the same church which partners with Marie Ens in working at the Military Hospital. Their partnership with FAITH is another aspect of their outreach. The FAITH project is working in partnership with the church in several areas of Phnom Penh where women are poor and have no income to support the family. The slum areas by the railway track and market-sellers are some of the poorest places that this church reaches with help in earning a living. Several of the congregation are formerly street children who have been given a home. Single mothers or widows who are HIV positive are being employed in a cashew nut processing plant where they can earn enough to eat.

Afterwards we visited a village helped by the project, which was composed of 75 households; 35 of these are headed by widows. This village was chosen because initially there was one household where there were believers, and it had been classified as a most difficult place to work. Many other NGOs had tried to work there without success. The village headman had said the people were lazy and would not help themselves.

FAITH did not expect to have quick results but they never gave up on villages that clearly needed help. The work began initially with a children's outreach followed by mothers showing an interest, so they began to teach them basic health and hygiene such as washing your hands before a meal and the necessity of cleaning teeth. It was hard to continue with little response but Milet felt strongly that she and her team needed to show the love of Christ to needy people and to love them unconditionally as he taught us to do.

The village experienced a drought followed by floods and they had no food to eat. The FAITH team then told them they would help them if they were prepared to help themselves.

They depended on the land for a source of income and when it did not produce a harvest they sold it to money lenders. When they became sick they borrowed from the same lenders to pay for medicines and the interest rates left them penniless. This state of affairs left them to work when they could, on land that at one time was their own property. When FAITH was able to help them to see the root of their problems it was much easier to motivate them to help themselves. The soil in the village was poor, so the yield from it was low. This was due to deforestation in the nearby mountain regions.

After weekly visits to establish good relations with these villagers and instruct them in simple Bible teaching, progress began slowly. They established a rice bank for the community and showed the people how to build the barn using it as a storage place when they did have a yield from the land. They discovered that the village chief, who had said the villagers were lazy, was the man who lent money at exorbitant interest rates! The chief was informed that FAITH had permission from the government and they were in partnership with the Minister of Rural Development together with EFC. Wisdom and skill in careful discussions made all the difference and the village started on the long road to development and improved living.

Setting up a revolving loan system enabled the people to buy chickens and pigs and so produce some food. The one Christian lady who was attending Bible school in Phnom Penh was actually the former wife of a village chief who was murdered. Politically this country is still a volatile place and it is not uncommon for a political opponent to be shot in order to gain power. Despite the circumstances this lady remained strong in her faith and began to hold Bible studies and teach praise songs to the other villagers. There is no electricity in this village so the little fellowship group began in candlelight. As the houses are constructed in simple wood and thatch, sound carries. Some opposed these meetings at first but after receiving love and care from the FAITH team regularly, there are now 50 of these people attending the simple church that has been built near the clean waterwell FAITH provided.

The evangelising has not been done by the FAITH project but has sprung out of a desire of the ex-village chief's widow to spread the good news of the gospel. However all the FAITH staff have attended the Phnom Penh Bible school or the Baptist Convention. The team of workers were chosen if they had been in a leadership position in their own churches and showed a real desire to serve Christ. Once trained by FAITH, they had the development skills taught them so they could help the poor. The village chief was not happy about all this, so Milet had a talk with him and showed him respect, but at the same time gave him an invitation to attend the training sessions in Phnom Penh.

The church is now growing rapidly and the EFC was approached to come and help with the leadership and put in place someone who was Khmer but not involved with project work. A neighbouring community had a church from the Khmer Presbyterian group so the same group came on board to help this village. They have their own system of teaching sound Bible truths which is necessary as the church is only two years old.

There has been a period of persecution and problems. One lady who became a Christian had her motorbike stolen and there was an attempt made to burn down the church. The village people have now been taught to resolve their problems, to help themselves in development and to speak for themselves. Some of them thought the attack may have come from the village chief but all his children are now Christians and only one family remains without faith in Christ. The latest development is that the village chief himself is now currently attending training at the New Jerusalem Church.

Indeed, the rice bank had a cross put on the door as a symbol of gratitude to God for providing for their needs. There were vegetable gardens producing a variety of vegetables, cows were grazing and sitting in the shade of a mango tree, chewing the cud. Women washed their clothes at the well and the pretty children were enjoying a swim and splash in a nearby pond full of water lilies and lotus flowers. Across the bright green rice paddyfields were sugar palm trees and distant mountains in a brilliant blue sky combining to make the landscape one of great beauty and tranquillity. There had been a good rainfall promising a harvest of plentiful rice.

When FAITH started to work in this village in the year 2000 there was only one family who were believers; later on key people turned to Christ, especially the widow of the former village chief. One elderly lady feels she cannot attend the church as her son is a monk in the nearby Buddhist temple, but she recently broke a bone following a motorbike accident and she was confined to her bed. The FAITH team went to visit her and asked if they could pray with her. The village believers have made a decision themselves to ask the EFC if their church can be a member.

Already this church of 74 households is experiencing persecution. In the next village where the market takes place they are banning the Christians from selling their produce. As this village is being prospered the next village may have been very angry with them but they are beginning to ask if there is a possibility of the FAITH project helping them! The FAITH project has been a 'pilot project' in a research programme but in 2005 when it is given the resources it may well help the next village too. Meanwhile because the Christians have been banned from selling their produce they are learning to look after the poor elsewhere in giving some of their excess to the next village. This is helping them to show the love of Christ and witness to the provision of God in their lives.

In the year 2000 a survey was done in the village as to how many could read and write and only seven could read so there is now an increasing call for a school in the village. The only school in the area is too far away for the children to travel. This necessity for a school is currently being placed before the church in order to find the resources. The people have agreed to help with the building, but teachers need to be government trained to give the children the needed education. Milet is confident that as God has provided every need for this village so far, he will continue to help and provide this facility too.

One FAITH member joined the project in 2000 on secondment from a church in Phnom Penh. He was brought up in a poor family with several brothers and sisters. Being the second oldest, he went into the city to find work to help support the family during the time when the UNTAC forces were supervising the elections, and the 'red light' district greatly increased. The family lived in an area where there was a church. He attended the church spasmodically and at that time he did not have a job; so the pastor, anxious to help him, offered some small jobs in decorating and building works in the church. Through this act of kindness, he became a Christian and his life was transformed. He attended the Baptist Convention Course, which is a year-long leadership training course and he matured and was raised to a leadership position in the church.

At the time he joined FAITH he was outstanding in his contribution to the local church. He had a wife and two children, but his health started to deteriorate in 2003. He became sick with typhoid and there are facilities in Phnom Penh to have this treated. The team saw that he had the best health care but he did not recover from the typhoid although he was on the right medicine. Finally he was admitted to hospital and the results of his blood tests showed he was HIV positive. When Milet gently told him this, he was terribly upset. He felt dreadfully ashamed of this fact, and humiliated that he had brought such dishonour on the church, his family and his father. He was found dead only a few days afterwards.

Milet felt that this one incident must raise a challenge to the churches as they generally see AIDS as God's punishment on the people, so why hinder his punishment? Sixty per cent of the population are young people. How many of them will be converted after they have had 'a fling'? They will belong to Christ when they are forgiven, so the church will have to face these issues with the compassion of Christ. In Buddhist society sometimes the father of a prospective bridegroom will introduce his son to a prostitute before the wedding. The Cambodian church is still a young church but as the younger and older generation become Christians these are issues that have to be faced with sensitivity yet maintaining biblical principles. Men have always led lives of promiscuity in Cambodian society but women have not even had a voice on any of these issues. In the villages that Milet has helped, many of the women have lost their husbands through AIDS and they are often HIV positive too, though they are unaware of this, sometimes for years.

Milet left this appeal, that if Jesus were here today how would he respond to these issues? Our biblical basis is the great commandment of Jesus, to love God with all your heart, mind and strength. The new Christians do this. They meet for praise and worship, often daily, but that is only half of the command. The other half is to love your neighbour as yourself. That is the difficult issue but it is still a part of the commandment. If your neighbour is hungry or has HIV how will you love your neighbour in those situations? Again it is a challenge to the church. If we want to be Christians only in words, but our lives don't show them that same love in deeds, how can we expect people to turn from Buddhism to Christianity? We must proclaim the gospel but we must also practise the teachings of love and care in our practical lives.

Milet had done her own survey on the church growth, looking at the different ministries; the highest priority is evangelism; discipleship was one of the low concepts. There is a danger of the church growing fast in numbers but not in quality. When low morality has been part of the culture of a nation, discipleship must be a strong factor in a growing church.

Milet has experience in these serious issues and is now assisting Revd Heng Cheng on the board of the Evangelical Fellowship of Cambodia. This beautiful, former orphan girl from the Philippines, who had to survive personal tragedy to support her own brother and sisters in those difficult years has been polished and shaped for this time in Cambodia. Running her home with utmost efficiency, it is a place to relax and feel loved; her husband praises her. 'A wife of noble character who can find? She is worth far more than rubies. Her husband has full confidence in her and lacks nothing of value. She brings him good, not harm, all the days of her life … She opens her arms to the poor and extends her hands to the needy … She speaks with wisdom, and faithful instruction is on her tongue. She watches over the affairs of her household and does not eat the bread of idleness' (Prov. 31:10–12,20,26,27).

Remembering that her mother had died when she was only fifty has made Milet value every year she is given to serve the Lord. Milet recognises this: 'I see the need for my life to be a model for others to follow. I have 14 members of staff, and if they are to walk rightly with God they need to be able to see my lifestyle as one they can copy. In this way I will have impacted their lives and I hope the lives of their friends and relatives too.'

The same message was given at the Pastors Graduation Ceremony at Barnabas' church. This inspiring day was held at the same time as the Water Festival which is a Buddhist feast and national holiday. The large auditorium was packed to the door. Musicians were playing praise songs while children danced in Khmer dress. There was an air of great celebration, far greater than any of the Buddhist events. Most of the people were dressed in traditional Khmer costumes which are colourful and elegant at the same time. It was a long but joyful occasion and 33 newly trained pastors were dedicated to serve the Lord. Many of these would leave the comparative comforts of city dwelling and preach the gospel in more spartan rural areas. One guarantee they would have was the loving, caring, prayerful backing of Barnabas and his wife Boury. Barnabas travels throughout the provinces to be a shepherd to the shepherds and his great love for his flock was the dominant feature of the day.

Revd Heng Cheng gave a word of encouragement and this was followed by a challenging address by Dr Russell Bowers from World Vision (also a Baptist minister and theologian). He spoke from 1 Timothy 4: 'The Spirit … says that in later times some will abandon the faith … point these things out to the brothers, you will be a good minister of Christ Jesus … Command and teach these things … set an example for the believers in speech, in life, in love, in faith and in purity …Be diligent in these matters … Watch your life and doctrine closely … Persevere in them, because if you do, you will save both yourself and your hearers' (vv. 1,6,11,12,15,16).

He asserted how false teachers had arrived in Cambodia, and these new pastors were to warn their flock about them and live their lives according to the teachings of the Bible. They were commanded to teach sound doctrine as the church is still young, and needs to put down roots in the word. The most essential part of their work was that they should be a model of the faith in their lives. The best gift they could give their church was the example of their own lifestyle. Ten years had gone by since the beginning of the rapid growth of the church in Cambodia. In 1993 the dying embers of the church were fanned into life and it had grown numerically at a great rate, praise God, but it is still a needy church. Paul was the greatest church planter of all time. He wrote these instructions to Timothy as he was passing on the baton to a younger man so that he followed in his footsteps. The pastors were challenged:

Are you going to be such an example that you can ask your people to follow in your footsteps?

There are examples in the Old and New Testament of people who started well and then got side-tracked. We love the psalms of David and his great victories in battle but he was caught by the greatest temptation you will face – yes, all of you. Keep your thoughts and life pure, don't indulge in impure thoughts nor be taken captive by a beautiful woman. David was at ease when this temptation overtook him; he confesses his sin and is forgiven but from that moment in the life of David, it became a downward spiral. Thereafter we read of all the things that happened in his family and as king. He had compromised the faith and his victories were never the same after that. First of all don't let your armour slip in areas of sexual temptation.

The second area of temptation is in integrity with money. There is a lot of temptation in this area especially where there is great poverty. Absolute integrity is required of a leader. Don't let the love of money mark you and be content with what you have got.

Daniel is an example in the Old Testament whose life was beyond reproach. Your congregation will watch your life and example. Let it be like Daniel's that when they look for something that is not right they will never find an inconsistency. Your personal prayer time and reading of the word must never be eroded by being too busy with pastoral work.

Don't take on too much so that you do not have time to be alone with God and read and listen to his voice. In the early church, as in Cambodia today, there are practical needs to be met; but put in place faithful men who will take care of these issues. Jesus found a place of refuge himself during his earthly ministry, in the home of Mary and Martha. Wouldn't all of you like to have Jesus come into your house? And a true answer would be, after you have considered whether you would be prepared for him to see everything in your house. Keep a balance in your life. You want to set a banquet for the Lord and provide for every need, but not at the expense of spending time with him.

Never neglect a close walk with the Lord. It is vital if you are to have a fruitful ministry. Be diligent in these matters; give yourself wholly to them so that everyone will see your progress. They will be unable to see your progress if you compromise on purity of life, integrity with money and lack reading the word and being in company with Christ. Then we all need to persevere in these things because it is a lifetime's work to watch your life and doctrine closely. Many are left behind because they fail to watch their lives closely. It is a wonderful ministry to be called into and if you persevere you will be blessed of the Lord and your life will be a blessing to others as well. Demas was taken on by Paul to help in the ministry, but later we read that he had forsaken Paul, having loved the present age. Start well, persevere, keep pure, be honest, be marked by integrity and grow in the faith so that all can see it. The best gift you can give your church is an example they can follow.

CHAPTER TWENTY:

Poverty to Palaces

Great strides forward in the rebuilding of Cambodia have been made but there is still a long way to go. We have seen how the ministry of WEC International, through Jim and Agnes Verner has helped to strengthen the young church but in addition to this, WEC has a team leadership of five people, one of whom is Timothee Paton involved in helping the poorest of the poor on the streets of Phnom Penh. There are approximately 20 helpers from different countries and they have an outreach twice weekly to children and families living or working on the streets. After meeting up for a time of prayer, teams of three people including a Khmer speaker go out on a tuk tuk (a Cambodian three-wheeler mode of small transport) to a specific area of the city with bags of clothes, shoes and food, as well as gospel booklets. Each time they see street children or people collecting rubbish, they stop the vehicle. Clothes and food are shared not as an end in itself but as a means of contact and introduction. They bring the gospel into the talk and encourage them to attend a church close by. As they discover why they are on the street they challenge them to consider a better life.

Beside the outreach times, they do the necessary follow-up on those who have requested their help. As a result children are brought to schools and provided with uniforms and supplies, sick people are taken to the doctor or the hospital, homeless mothers and children are introduced to a shelter and some street kids are given the opportunity to live in foster homes or an orphanage. Others are accompanied to attend a local church service and introduced to the Christian community. Homeless families are provided with housing and visited regularly.

Tim has some challenges daily and one day he was woken at 2.32 a.m. by a phone call. 'It's a girl!' announced the father, an AIDS sufferer living on the streets of Phnom Penh. His wife had just given birth to their fourth child, right there on the pavement. When Tim visited the family he saw the beautiful little girl sleeping under a mosquito net on a plank of wood above their rubbish cart. In the afternoon he helped them find a new home with a Catholic mission.

A week later a phone call at 7.30 a.m. alerted Tim to the plight of six more street families. The police were trying to move them on and confiscate the carts the families used for collecting recyclable items from rubbish bags. With his Khmer co-worker, Tim went to help but when he arrived the police had left – without taking the carts. At 9.30 a.m. Tim and his co-worker found a landlady willing to let small houses on the outskirts of the city. The houses were in an ideal spot with a school nearby and a safe place for the children to play.

When the landlady saw the procession of 24 street people (all extremely poor and some very sick) plus a dog coming into her compound, she had second thoughts. When told that they were all regular church-goers, she said, 'I am a Christian too, I would not have rented my houses if these people were not believers.' By the time Tim had left the compound the children had already cleaned their new home. He wondered how long it was since the families slept under a roof. Two weeks later, the landlady changed her mind about having so many 'dirty people' in her compound. Perhaps the neighbours complained. But the Lord had another place for them, right in the centre of the city. Every Sunday a Khmer pastor picks them up for church. The new landlord is very kind and plans to build four extra rooms for other families living on the streets.

There is much to give thanks for in progress being made to help the poorest of the poor but the work is a long haul. However several more families have been housed and there are several Christian NGOs helping children. New Life Church, pastored by Chuck McCaul, which has a large outreach to the younger generation, is now running a weekly programme attended by dozens of street children. Some 15 of the young people of the church are leading this meeting. On International Children's Day the EFC held an event for children and several other organisations are seeing the needs. Some of the street people are not ready for a change of life but the Cambodian church has begun to catch the vision to reach out to their own people.

There is still a great need for helpers among the street children and the homeless. Estimates suggest that there are up to 15,000 street children in Phnom Penh. Some are homeless and orphaned while others spend long hours collecting rubbish along the road to support their families. Many street children and workers have no home, no education, no medical care and are malnourished and extremely vulnerable to exploitation from the sex industry. Many are addicted to toxic substances (from glue sniffing to taking stronger drugs), getting involved in gang activity and petty theft. However, the good news is that many are responding to the gospel message and are seeking a new life. In the eyes of the world these are nobodies but in God's sight they are gems.

We now move from the scenes of abject poverty to the magnificent royal palace, built in traditional Khmer architecture on the banks of the Tonle Sap river in Phnom Penh. King Norodom Sikanouk is revered as a god-king by his subjects and his presence has doubtless brought a measure of stability. On 8 October 2004 he shocked his subjects by offering his abdication, potentially ending a reign – some spent in exile – which saw everything from independence struggles to the Khmer Rouge genocide. Prince Rannaridh said the declaration left Cambodia like a family where the children have no father, and like a house without a roof, adding that it was very shocking for all Cambodians who love him and regard him as sacred. But the king had threatened abdication several times before, often during political crises.

Sihanouk's successor is meant to be chosen after his death by a nine-member Throne Council, and it was thought that the announcement by the king could be a way he was able to have influence in the selection. The eighty-two-year-old king made a statement, in which he said he was too old, sick and tired to continue. He said he had had great honour to serve the nation and people for more than half a century, but asked all compatriots to please allow him to retire.

On 30 October at the royal palace, King Norodom Sihamoni was crowned king. The choice surprised everyone as he is little known to his subjects. King Norodom Sihamoni, a shaven-headed former ballet dancer, did not initially want the job but was unanimously elected by the Royal Throne Council. At the culmination of two days of religious ceremonies, King Sihamoni arrived in the throne hall of the royal palace, to the sounds of conch shells. Wearing a white uniform with gold-embroidered cuffs and epaulettes and bejewelled insignia, he swore the oath 3 times as 52 Buddhist monks chanted blessings.

No crown was placed on his head but with replicas of the royal regalia at his side – most of the originals disappeared after his father was deposed in an American-backed coup in 1970 – he had 'holy water' poured over his head. King Sihamoni described the event as an immense honour and went on to say that he would devote his body and soul to the service of the people and the nation.

King Sihamoni, fifty-one, is unmarried and has spent most of his life abroad. He was kept under house arrest with his father while the Khmer Rouge regime murdered an estimated 1.7 million Cambodians in the late 1970s. After the Khmer Rouge were ousted by a Vietnamese invasion, he went into exile in China and has spent most of the past 20 years in Paris as a dancer, professor of dance and as Cambodia's ambassador to UNESCO. A softly spoken man, he is described as quiet, simple and private. Highly artistic, he lived modestly in France, occupying a discreet apartment and often eschewing his official UNESCO car in favour of the Metro.

King Sihamoni's most important role will be to fulfil the crown's role as a focus of continuity and stability in a country ravaged by war, genocide and poverty. After the coronation ceremony he walked out of the throne room arm-in-arm with Hun Sen, Cambodia's prime minister and his half-brother Prince Norodom Rannaridh, president of the national assembly and leader of the opposition FUNCIPEC party, but he will have to tread a difficult path between them in future. It will be interesting to see if he maintains the same tradition of his father in meeting with the EFC leaders annually for prayer.

The amazing goodness and grace of God has been demonstrated in the Anlong Veng area. This was the biggest stronghold of Pol Pot and his feared Khmer Rouge soldiers. No one dared to visit this area as it had a reputation for violence, killings and no outside contact with the world. It was freed from the Khmer Rouge in 1998 but the enforced atheism of the communists created an atmosphere of hopelessness, and statistics gathered in 2000 indicated 65 per cent of the residents were illiterate.

Despite the forebodings of this formidable area, Cambodian Christians were burdened to establish a witness for Christ. After a time of prayer, an indigenous ministry sent a team of missionaries and church planters to Anlong Veng. The Lord has richly blessed their work and there are now seven churches, a home and school for orphaned children and those who have made a commitment to Christ are former officers of the once-feared Khmer Rouge. Two of Pol Pot's most relied-upon military leaders are church leaders. One of these former Khmer Rouge leaders has a wife who will soon be employed in the orphanage. This is a remarkable outpouring of the power of Christ to transform the lives of these killers into messengers of the gospel of forgiveness. Some are sceptical and wary still as they cannot understand this kind of forgiveness so this new breakthrough needs prayer support that it will continue to be the beam of hope in the darkest area.

CHAPTER TWENTY-ONE:

Mountains of Jewels:
Ratanakiri

Following all the tragedies and violence that has marked this land in the past, we see how good and gracious is our God who comes to the aid of his people when they cry to him. Areas of Cambodia that had no clean water, no food and no hope are now being transformed by the work of those who have been called to rebuild the 'broken walls' of this nation. When Nehemiah asked about the plight of the people of God after their exile he was told:

> 'Those who survived the exile and are back in the province are in great trouble and disgrace. The wall of Jerusalem is broken down, and its gates have been burned with fire.' When I heard these things, I sat down and wept. For some days I mourned and fasted and prayed before the God of heaven. (Neh.1:3,4)

Cambodia has been a place of tears and the people who have been used greatly by God to rebuild the 'broken walls' have done so, often in tears and fasting. It has been a costly enterprise but there are jewels that are emerging from the darkest places to shine as representatives of the Light of the World, bringing new hope and the promise of eternal life out of their dark experiences.

As this fledgling church began to grow and spread its wings, it has faced obstacles and predators. Fledgling birds have the constant vigilance of a watchful parent to assist their flight from the nest. This young church has had its trials and difficulties, but God set his heart on this land to bless it through the ministry of his chosen servants. Revd Heng Cheng, pastors Barnabas and Paul, Steve Westergren, Marie Ens, Nigel and Milet Goddard, Brian Maher, Marie Hill, Reaksa and there are without doubt many more who have contributed to the growth of this church. Jim and Agnes Verner were put through hardships and trials in Thailand that enabled them to have the needed wisdom to help other missionaries and some of the national leaders to set up disciplinary action when it was needed, shepherd care, loving compassion, yet firm obedience to the directions given in the word of God, that has enabled the church to put down roots in the faith.

Stories of some of the jewels that I have been privileged to meet are in the pages of this book. But there are many others I have not met and countless hidden gems that will only be brought to light on that final day when God makes up his jewels.

Pearls of wisdom and spiritual insight were needed in the province of Ratanakiri (which means 'Mountains of Jewels'), where there was a rare gem that had been through the Refiner's fire before he arrived in Cambodia. He developed a 'Paul and Timothy' relationship with Jim Verner so let us see how God arranged his circumstances to bless the land and plant churches among its tribal groups.

The indigenous tribes of Ratanakiri

Gordon started work in Cambodia with the Mennonite Central Committee and his first assignment was in Takeo

Gordon of Ratanakiri

Province to protect, manage and replant the degraded forest land. At first he was reticent to make contact with any Christians because he had been through a frightening experience in a neighbouring communist country where his friendship with the local believers was drawn to the government's attention. They took action and he was subsequently asked to leave. However after a year in Takeo Province Gordon was led into a relationship with a small church in the village of Slaa, which means betel nut palm. The buds and blossoms of this tree are used as confetti in Khmer wedding celebrations.

Slaa was the home village of Ung Sam Oeun, one of the main characters of the account of the pre-Khmer Rouge era church told in *Anointed for Burial* written by Todd and DeAnne Burke (Seattle, Washington: Frontline Communications, 1989). Sam Oeun and his wife were martyred but his younger brother Ung Sophal went on to become the leader of Global Network in Phnom Penh. They helped Barnabas when he returned to the city from Site Two camp in 1993. The church in Slaa was pioneered by Sophal's sister and her husband in the difficult years of the eighties when it had to be underground. Gordon joined this little group and they met faithfully to pray for him and his work; some amazing things happened.

As they met for times of prayer and fasting, the Lord revealed some of his future plans for Cambodia and many of them have already come to pass. One of the promises given to this group was from Isaiah 60:

> Foreigners will re-build your walls, and their kings will serve you. Though in anger I struck you, in favour I will show you compassion … The glory of Lebanon will come to you, the pine, the fir, and the cypress together, to adorn the place of my sanctuary … Although you have been forsaken and hated, with no-one travelling through, I will make you the everlasting pride and joy of all generations … Instead of bronze, I will bring you gold, and silver in places of iron … No longer will violence be heard in your land, nor ruin or destruction within your borders, but you will call your walls Salvation and your gates Praise. (vv. 10,13,15,17,18)

From the time that promise was given things started to change even in the natural environment. The local communities were given the vision for protecting the forest which Gordon had come to replant. The same group were told to expect a miracle on the thirteenth day of the twelfth month from Esther 9:1: 'on the thirteenth day of the twelfth month … the edict commanded by the king was to be carried out'. Sure enough, on 13 December 1994 the Cambodian government made a hitherto unknown precedent, setting an agreement to hand over the forest land to the local communities for management and restoration. The fact that the Cambodian government had agreed to hand over this land was quite miraculous, because it was only just emerging from communism. Gordon's presence was important to augment this agreement as his speciality is in the field of forestry. The local community needed expert advice on how to maintain the area, but it was a remarkable act of divine intervention for the restoration of the land and forests to be part of God's plans to heal the land of Cambodia, just as he had promised all those years ago to his chosen people of Israel. The forestry project demonstrated that the degraded land and forest could be restored and allowed to harvest products for the local people's benefit.

The communities in Takeo Province had survived on a poor diet, with no clean water and few directions on how to use the land to grow good crops. Isaiah 41:17–20 was Gordon's promise that he received from the Lord for this area:

> The poor and needy search for water, but there is none; their tongues are parched with thirst. But I the LORD will answer them; I, the God of Israel, will not forsake them. I will make rivers flow on barren heights, and springs within the valleys. I will turn the desert into pools of water, and the parched ground into springs. I will put in the desert the cedar and the acacia, the myrtle and the olive. I will set pines in the wasteland, the fir and the cypress together, so that people may see and know, may consider and understand, that the hand of the LORD has done this, that the Holy One of Israel has created it.

During the period that Gordon was in Takeo the acacias and myrtles really were replanted and springs of water started to flow on barren heights. But none of this would have been possible without the faithful community of Christian believers, praying for Gordon and his work. There were others committed to pray for this gentle, quiet, unassuming servant of the Lord, who had been sent with an unusual mission to 'help rebuild the broken walls'.

In August 1994 the Lord impressed on Gordon that he was to leave MCC at the end of that year and then he would be given clear guidance what to do. During the six month waiting period Gordon developed a relationship with Pastor Barnabas and his wife Boury whose prayer support for the people of Ratanakiri was to prove invaluable. During the six month period, as he waited for direction, he had several offers of well-paid jobs but did not feel these were from the Lord; then a request came from a secular funding agency to co-ordinate a study of natural resources used by indigenous people in Ratanakiri Province. Feeling concerned about working for a non-Christian organisation, he was led to a scripture in Acts 10:20: 'Do not hesitate to go with them, for I have sent them.'

The contract for the new job started exactly six months after leaving MCC even to the day! Gordon met Jim and Agnes Verner in a church service in Phnom Penh after his first exploratory trip to Ratanakiri. This meeting was a 'divine appointment' as Gordon and the Verners were uniquely joined in the Spirit, and it was the beginning of a long-standing, spiritual mentoring relationship. Later, when Jim and Agnes were seeking the Lord (in early 1998) for a field of ministry, following on their pastoral service with SAO, Marie the artist and jeweller suggested they went to Ratanakiri.

The donor agency requested Gordon to start an organisation to assist the indigenous people of Ratanakiri to maintain control of the natural resources on which their livelihood depended. Since 1996, the work which Gordon had pioneered has enabled local communities to stand up for their rights to continue managing the forest and land which they have used and managed for generations. Both the land and the forest were under threat from business interests that wanted to cut down the forest and push the people off their land so they could start industrial plantations of coffee, rubber, cashew nuts and other cash crops. This pattern of development had been repeated in many countries, where indigenous people lost their homes and land. They ended up as nothing more than slave labourers for rich new owners, and in their sense of worthlessness they resorted to drugs, prostitution and other social ills. If this had succeeded in Ratanakiri, the pristine forest and natural scenic beauty would have been destroyed.

For the first few years Gordon played a low-key role in the church in Ban Lung, the provincial capital town which had the first Christian church in Ratanakiri that had sprung up on its own. It was started by an uncle and nephew who were Bunong tribal people from Mondulkiri, a neighbouring province. They had relatives in Vietnam who came to know the Lord during a revival of the hill-tribe people in the 1980s when they made a commitment to Christ. They brought the message with them to Ratanakiri and the Lord blessed this little church which had had no outside help. Sick people were healed and the Lord added to their numbers. They didn't know how to worship but one girl recounted how she became a Christian and somehow she immediately knew the worship songs. She was appointed to be a worship leader and today she continues as a gifted singer, together with being a literacy trainer with ICC. Another couple were converted after their child had been bitten by a poisonous snake. They went to the little group of believers who prayed for the child and he was healed so the whole family became Christians.

The nascent church received a boost in 1994 when a dental training programme (through an organisation now part of ICC) came to Ratanakiri. The church in Ban Lung helped to plant a new church among the Tampuen people in nearby Yiak Lom where there is a beautiful deep volcanic lake. At that time healings were quite common and many villagers became Christians because they felt God would protect their health. The translator of the ICC team was a gifted Cambodian evangelist, who was later to become son-in-law to Barnabas and Boury, as he married their daughter. He preached and taught in this small church to show them the way of salvation. ICC set up a development project for the highland communities in adult literacy, health and agriculture. They sent some of the leaders of the small churches to Phnom Penh for training and also brought leaders from the city to set up youth camps and conferences. Sometimes, the truths became distorted because of the language gaps and city leaders having a different world view. The minority tribes all spoke different languages, some of which had not been written down. ICC has developed a language research and literacy programme under agreements with the government.

The missing element was for real on-the-spot mentoring and guidance which the apostle Paul gave to the early church. As a result of the relationship Gordon had formed with Jim and Agnes Verner, on his visits to the city, he called on them to come and help in the many small indigenous churches and tribes who as yet had not heard the message. Everyone was excited about the Verners coming to Ratanakiri but God had different ideas. His plans were to take the church through a period of painful threshing and refining. Jim made several visits to Ratanakiri that enabled him to see the spiritual potential in Gordon and they were knitted together: Jim became Gordon's father in the Lord.

Gordon asked them to help an expatriate team with its church work and to solve some problems with some teams that needed wisdom to work together effectively. Jim met with the leaders and worked hard to bring about unity between the different parties. His wisdom and spiritual insight was recognised by the local churches and they asked him to consider going there on a full-time basis but with the other commitments Jim had in the Phnom Penh area this was not possible. However, Jim's meeting with the leaders in Ratanakiri resulted in organisations working harmoniously together and procedures were put into place for the necessary disciplinary measures to be taken with some elders in the church who were not acting rightly. Following all this Gordon regularly corresponded with the Verners and made frequent visits to their home for long talks and times of prayer.

There were other problems in the small indigenous churches that came to an impasse and even the national leaders could not help. Jim was able to convince Gordon that the structures he had put in place in similar situations all those years ago in Sukhothai Province, Thailand, would work in Cambodia to help the churches move forward. The Verners had planted the local 'Bonds of Fellowship' churches in Thailand which later developed into an association of 60 independent churches under strong indigenous leadership. These churches are thriving, growing churches today, so God had given Jim the needed wisdom from these early years of service that were used by God to unify and consolidate the indigenous churches of Ratanakiri Province.

For many years the Verners had prayed for the Kreung tribe who lived in Ratanakiri Province but had not heard the gospel message. Gordon had forged a good relationship with this tribal group by gaining support for their tribal minority rights, saving their future from unscrupulous businessmen and helping them to replant some of the forest areas and maintain their gardens that produce upland rice, dozens of varieties of vegetables, medicines and condiments. He facilitated a Kreung Christian from Ban Lung to bring the gospel message and this was also augmented by some of the national leaders coming alongside to help.

The Verners' first visit to a Kreung tribal village had left indelible memories. Access to the village was over deeply rutted roads made of volcanic lava which had hardened into rock. The area is one of great scenic beauty, with extinct volcanoes forming mountains with flat tops. The forests have very tall trees and the hills and streams have a unique beauty quite different from other areas of Cambodia. They walked round the village and observed the way of life. The houses were simple constructions of wood and thatch. In many of these homes there were very sick people lying on mats by the entrances. Nobody seemed to care about their welfare.

In the centre of the village was a meeting house in front of which was a circle of poles used on the occasion of buffalo sacrifices. These took place several times a year and were meant to appease the spirits. There was a sense in which the villagers felt suffering, blood and torture could be the only way of appeasing the spirits of the mountains, rivers and streams which had the power to cause sickness.

Sacrifices were held at certain times of the year and involved talking to a buffalo for a whole day before tying it to one of the central poles in front of the meeting house. Beginning the sacrifice, wine was sipped from clay jars, to the accompaniment of music from special brass kongs (gongs). The buffalo was cut with knives, beaten slowly and finally had its legs broken waiting for it to die.

Agnes wept 'God's tears' for this tribe after witnessing the sacrifice. She prayed and interceded for them that they might be released from these animistic customs and come into the knowledge of their Creator God. At the same time Barnabas' wife Boury also had a burden to intercede for this tribe. Barnabas had always had a heart for the tribes of Ratanakiri and Boury has a ministry of intercessory prayer, not just for her husband's ministry but also for all the needs of the Cambodian people. The far-reaching effects of Barnabas' ministry have benefited greatly from his wife having this intercessory prayer ministry. Gordon was soaking up Jim's ministry and his experiences of church planting gained in Thailand; while he fasted and prayed Jim laid hands on him to receive special gifts from the Spirit. Shortly afterwards the Verners left Cambodia for an extended period of church deputation in Ireland and Canada, but Gordon experienced great gifts in teaching that brought him from his low-key background role into a new one of intensive ministry to the Ratanakiri churches.

A great breakthrough came when a local Kreung Christian, known to Gordon, taught his people the message that the great Creator God of the mountains, the forests and the streams had sent his Son to be a sacrifice for their sins so that they could be cleansed, healed and forgiven. The Kreung tribal people made a decision to follow Christ. In 2004 Gordon's aunt from Australia visited Cambodia and stayed with the Verners. Gordon joined his aunt for a few days in Phnom Penh where they all prayed together for a blessing on the new converts from the Kreung tribe. As they prayed, Gordon's aunt, who has a ministry in the prophetic word, said she felt there was something hidden with this tribe. It was chained and bound and the Lord wanted it to be released.

They went to visit the tribe and the Kreung Christian leader heard the message from Gordon's aunt. He knew immediately that God was speaking into the tribal music

which had stopped when they were converted. The kongs
had been hidden away in a hut and never used from the
time of the tribe's conversion. Everyone agreed that these
kongs could be released, cleansed and used for praise to
the great Creator God. A conference of historic value was
held as tribal leaders all came together in Ratanakiri and
unanimously decided, for the first time in history, to use
their traditional musical instruments in Christian worship.
A cleansing ceremony followed in which these kongs,
previously used in buffalo sacrifices and demon worship,
would now belong to Jesus! That same day the kongs took
centre stage in a memorable celebration of praise and
worship to God. Their musical accompaniment to the
praises and worship of the redeemed tribe resounded
throughout the green valleys, beyond the dark forests to
the hills and mountains and it was all a wonderful answer
to the prayers of Agnes, Boury and the mission supporters
of Jim and Agnes who had been called to pray for this tribe.

Gordon's vision for the indigenous tribes of Ratanakiri
came from Isaiah 32:16–18:

> Justice will dwell in the desert and righteousness live in
> the fertile field. The fruit of righteousness will be peace;
> the effect of righteousness will be quietness and confidence
> for ever. My people will dwell in peaceful dwelling-places,
> in secure homes, in undisturbed places of rest.

All this has come to pass. When Jim Verner saw the
effectiveness of Gordon's ministry he laid hands on him for
continuing ministry in Ratanakiri. The Lord seemed to have
others to carry on the ministry in the north east with an
eminent Baptist teacher being of great help in establishing
good teaching together with the input of the NGOs.
Gordon regularly visits Jim for advice and mentoring and

they have developed a close relationship whereby the call to Ratanakiri that Jim had received at the WEC headquarters in 1965 (he had a specific call: Ratanakiri Province of Cambodia) has been passed on to Gordon.

Gordon lives in this remote province in a simple wooden house built on stilts made from local timber, with intermittent electricity supplies from a hydroelectric power station. When there is no electricity he has deliveries of ice to keep his food supplies fresh. It is still a very remote and hilly province, unlike other areas of Cambodia. Ratanakiri, 'Mountains of Jewels', describes the natural beauty of the forest and hills, as well as the rich mineral resources of gold and precious gems below the surface. But the metaphorical uncut diamonds are the 'minority peoples', the indigenous tribes with eight different language groups: the Kreung, Tampuen, Jarai, Kachok, Kavet, Preuv, Lun and Bunong, each distinct in their culture and way of life and different from the lowland Khmer people. The forests contain wildlife including tiger, deer, Asian elephants, scaly anteaters, loris and monkeys, monitor lizards, plus hundreds of varieties of natural fish and freshwater turtles in the streams.

Brian Maher told me of a little gathering of tribal people in Mondulkiri Province that had heard the Christian message through FEBC broadcasts. They knew of no missionaries or other believers so just met together to listen to the radio broadcasts. They had no Bibles or song books and had no idea how to start a church but when missionaries went to this area they were surprised to find these believers already loving the Lord Jesus but having no knowledge of how to build a church. Jim and Agnes Verner went for short periods to help these indigenous people and some of the pastors trained by Barnabas in Site Two camp also went into remote villages to encourage and help to build churches based on sound biblical teaching.

In 1998 Gordon facilitated six indigenous church leaders to receive three month's intensive training with Barnabas in his School of Practical Ministries. This was called the 'church planters' programme where participants receive training in leadership, character, as well as administration and evangelism. (It was the graduation day of this school that I attended.) After returning to Ratanakiri they helped to train others and to initiate outreach from each local church. Other tribal groups were reached by Jarai Christians coming over the border from Vietnam because of the severe persecution from the communist government there. As these churches grew they needed help with teaching and CAMA sent one of their teachers to disciple the Jarai leaders through their Theological Training by Extension. This teacher is now the head of the CAMA youth programme for the whole of Cambodia.

In December 1997, revival broke out in eastern Ratanakiri near the Vietnam border. Several churches were planted among the Jarai people and this was purely the result of their Jarai counterparts and relatives in Vietnam coming across the border because of persecution of their Christian faith by the communist authorities in Vietnam. The Jarai tribal groups were evangelised by CAMA missionaries in the 1960s. After the communist takeover in Vietnam, the churches grew at a phenomenal rate. By the end of the 1980s 30 per cent of the Jarai in Vietnam had become Christians.

One village near the Vietnam border in Ratanakiri had their first convert in December 1997. From that small beginning the church grew to 350 people in the space of one year. It caused considerable consternation to the authorities in Vietnam as well as those in Ratanakiri! Until recently the Jarai churches had been subject to discrimination by the Cambodian authorities, as well as continual surveillance by the secret police from Vietnam (who suspect them of harbouring refugees fleeing persecution in Vietnam). In 2001 the church in Lom village that had grown so rapidly was closed by the authorities. This action could have been contested under the Cambodian constitution, but the leaders chose rather to follow the example of their Lord and Master who 'did not open his mouth' (see Is. 53:7). The church divided into seven underground house churches, and continued to grow. Unable to find any fault, the authorities lifted their ban on public meetings in 2002, and the church has continued to expand numerically in Lom village. Their real need now is for deep biblical teaching.

In May 1999, the Jarai churches in Ratanakiri came under the care of the CAMA in Cambodia, who sent a Cambodian missionary from Battambang Province to provide teaching and care for the Jarai leaders. This couple sowed their lives into the work and were a great help in the Jarai churches. So we see how God is interested in the indigenous people and he had plans for them. 'Just as I watched over them to uproot and tear down, and to overthrow, destroy and bring disaster, so I will watch over them to build and to plant' (Jer. 31:28).

There has been a valuable contribution to the work in Ratanakiri by foreign mission, and extensive literacy work undertaken by ICC. They have developed a writing system for the Kreung language, prepared teaching materials which are widely used in the tribe today. An eminent Baptist minister has focused on developing an alphabet and dictionary for the Tampuen language. He was outstanding in his concern, practical help and shepherd care when the Ban Lung church went through a difficult time, due to in-fighting and jealousy. He provided temporary spiritual leadership until the church could get back on its feet again.

The message of salvation is spreading to these tribes and animal sacrifices are ceasing to exist. The Kreung tribal Christians now go out on a Sunday afternoon to evangelise other minority tribes. Because Gordon was working with a non-Christian organisation this actually had the effect of the local churches growing from their own experiences of seeing healings and other miracles; then the national leaders coming in to help, augmented by the Verners' care and wisdom.

There have been various strands, threads and chains of gold that have been used to display the jewels, pearls and gemstones of Ratanakiri. Tribal missionaries from Vietnam who suffered the fires of persecution, national leaders whose lives had been through hardship and pain, Khmer missionaries from the hopelessness of Site Two camp, being touched by the love of Christ; foreign missionaries who had given up the comforts of western living, development agencies with foreign Christians who gave up all their spare time to nurture the young church: all these threads have contributed, but none can claim ownership of the jewels of Ratanakiri.

So neither he who plants nor he who waters is anything, but only God, who makes things grow. The man who plants and the man who waters have one purpose, and each will be rewarded according to his own labour. For we are God's fellow-workers; you are God's field, God's building. By the grace God has given me, I laid a foundation as an expert builder, and someone else is building on it. But each one should be careful how he builds. For no-one can lay any foundation other than the one already laid, which is Jesus Christ. If any man builds on this foundation using gold, silver, costly stones, wood, hay or straw, his work will be shown for what it is, because the Day will bring it to light.' (1 Cor. 3:6–13)

CHAPTER TWENTY-TWO:

The Pearl of Great Price

Jewels and gemstones are still being mined from the mountains of Ratanakiri, but there are also precious gems being formed to shine eternally, perhaps to adorn the walls of the Holy City, the new Jerusalem that we read about in Revelation 21:2–4. The apostle John was an old man when he saw this amazing vision, and he tells us of the loud voice he heard saying, 'Now the dwelling of God is with men, and he will live with them … and be their God. He will wipe every tear from their eyes. There will be no more death or mourning or crying or pain, for the old order of things has passed away.' This glimpse into the world to come is the greatest hope for the nation of Cambodia, a place of tears that on that day will all be wiped away.

The great eternal God is working out his purposes for the universe and we finite beings only see a small fraction of those purposes in our short life-span. His plans are beyond our comprehension yet his promises are sure and they will come to pass in his time. The future for the redeemed is a glorious reality and in the eternal city the tree of life bears leaves that will be for the healing of this nation and all the other lands of this earth that are passing through tragedies.

Steve Westergren believes that God had set his heart on this land 80 years ago, and indeed he did, as Revd and Mrs Hammond arrived in Phnom Penh to begin the arduous task of translating the first Bible in 1923. They arrived with

Mr and Mrs David Ellison who went to preach the gospel, beginning in Battambang Province in a small village of rice farmers. The first church was planted there in obscurity, but it was one of the hidden jewels. When the Hammonds finished their task, Steve's father Cliff Westergren took over and brought the translated Bible to New York and had it printed under the direction of Revd Hammond.

Others were becoming aware of the needs of Cambodia and at the WEC headquarters, England in 1943 Leslie Brierley was asked by Norman Grubb, the general secretary, to make a world survey on the unreached peoples of that time. He reported that there were millions of Cambodians who had not heard the good news. In 1959 Leslie was commissioned to provide an update of the world survey and it took two years to compile. 'The Challenge of the Unachieved' was read at the conference of WEC leaders in 1961. Leslie, who is ninety-two, responded with great alacrity to my request for information on that report.

It stated, 'The C&MA pioneered this field in 1923, and up to 1961 were the only mission to work in the country. A vigorous well-rounded work has developed, but the field is hard and unresponsive. The CAMA pursues a vigorous literature policy … large editions of the gospels of Luke and John were printed for Bible Society. Twice daily broadcasts of thirty minutes gospel were prepared in their studio. One must first of all comment on the balance and poise of the Alliance programme, surely a model for any missionary! Evangelism, training, indigenous principles, translation work, literature production and distribution, radio, all have a part in the full-orbed design! Yet the hardness of the field is reflected in the paucity of results – less than a thousand in a population of five million, with at least three whole provinces without a single church group, and probably half the population unreached. The CAMA concluded their latest report by saying: "Cambodia continues to be very much the same hard, unproductive soil that it has been in the past. Probably the words of Francis Xavier of old best express the heart cry of God's servants in Cambodia, 'O Rock, O Rock! when wilt thou open?'" WEC felt there might be a contribution they could make by helping in the work amongst the primitive animist tribes people of the North East, as yet not reached by the gospel.'

In 1961 Leslie read the paper which covered points that he wanted WEC to take as a priority. Twelve more fields had been opened but six more ought to be opened by the Diamond Jubilee of the Mission (1973). Cambodia was one of the countries Leslie asked WEC to target. His report, 'The Challenge of the Unachieved' was read by Jim Verner and through it God called Jim to work in Cambodia. 'WEC did not achieve entry until 1993 but God always has his time for such matters as we have learnt in our pioneer work worldwide', was Leslie's comment on this.

Leslie made a short visit to Cambodia in 1965 and his description of that visit makes good reading

As I knew no one, I stayed in a rather seedy hotel until I found a French representative of CAMA who kindly offered me accommodation in their headquarters. Walking round the city of Phnom Penh I found myself in Monivong Road and noticed a nice church building with a cross at the top. It looked like a Protestant church. But alas, when I went to open the gate and enter, there was a huge padlock firmly locked, forbidding any entry.

During the few days I was able to stay I picked up a few things:- A fortune teller was doing business in the market, with the signs of the Zodiac decorating his stall; he would read hands and bumps on the head. He asked me to join his circle but of course I refused ... I was able to pick up

FEBA broadcasts from Bangalore. A Chinese church elder informed me there were only eight or nine Cambodian pastors in the country; there being so few Christians, that they could not afford to pay a pastor. Four of the pastors were in jail, I was told, but whilst there, they had managed to lead nine others to the Lord, 'more than they would have done outside the prison,' he said. The French CAMA representative informed me that the provinces still not evangelised were Svay Rieng, Stung Treng, Kompong Som, Posat, Mondulkiri and Ratanakiri.

Leslie's vision to see these provinces evangelised has been fulfilled, probably even beyond his wildest dreams. It has all been arranged by a sovereign God through a wide variety of channels. Every servant of Christ who has impacted this country has been a different channel of blessing because God is a God of diversity, not uniformity. Jim and Agnes are still serving their Master in ways he has designed, that has enabled them to be Christ's ambassadors in many areas and situations. They initiated the inception of the EFC and remained on its Executive Committee four years. Its vast outreach to the whole country must be attributed to God's sovereign work. Paul of Cambodia, Pastor Barnabas, Revd Heng Cheng have been mightily used by the Lord and now Milet Goddard will be bringing her skills to assist Revd Heng Cheng, and steer the FAITH project in the right direction.

The Verners never forget their time on the Tonle Sap lake, the input into Ratanakiri, the Khmer School of Language, Prek Hoo teaching teens, the KSL Mercy Home, but these are small pages in God's larger book, the final chapter of which has not yet been written. Jim still delights in preaching but he concentrates on being available for hurting people or complex situations. 'Tomorrow is too late if they need us today', is his view.

God set his heart on this land 80 years ago, when the ground was hard and rocky. In the mystery of his ways that are beyond our understanding, the Khmer Rouge broke up that hard rocky land, but their philosophies would have totally destroyed the whole nation if God had not intervened. Above the tide of evil that swept this beautiful land was the God of time and eternity who was looking for that pearl of great price. In Matthew 13:45 we read, 'Again, the kingdom of heaven is like a merchant looking for fine pearls. When he found one of great value, he went away and sold everything he had and bought it.' Pearls are formed because pain and constant irritation comes from a small particle of grit inside the oyster. It has the God-given ability to produce nacre to cover the grit and produce this beauty out of suffering. To redeem humankind and prepare a bride for Christ, God was prepared to suffer as he saw his only Son die on a cruel cross and shed his blood for our redemption. The bride, the wife of the Lamb, will be presented to Christ in that coming day, shining with jewels that have been formed in suffering. I love to think of the redeemed church of God in all her beauty and diversity of nations, tribes and peoples being like that pearl of great price in the sight of God.

The forests and jungles of Ratanakiri were the base from which the Khmer Rouge conducted their warfare. From this place of beauty came the most dreadful warfare of the twentieth century. The Khmer Rouge cut down the forests to provide illegal timber for money and the jewels of Ratanakiri were being mined and sold by the evil soldiers of the communist army in order to purchase landmines and other weapons of warfare to kill and destroy. From their base situated in the mountains and jungles they carried on their guerrilla warfare throughout the whole of Cambodia. These jewels from the mountains of Ratanakiri were also used to fund the warfare against the Vietnamese occupation bringing more misery, suffering and death.

Phnom Penh, when it is translated means 'a monument to the dead' and Kampuchea, the name given to Cambodia in these terrible times means 'the land that can never be healed'. Today sapphires, zircons, rubies and gold and precious gemstones are being mined from these mountains giving employment to local people. To mine these precious jewels is a costly enterprise. Workers dig wells down steep shafts into the mountainside, the shafts go into the dark earth which has to be sifted to find the jewels. Rubies, sapphires and zircons are in the dark depths of the earth; they were formed through the heat and pressure of volcanic eruptions thousands of years ago. The precious resources of timber and jewels were wasted in warfare but are now producing income for the people who work there. There are now uncut diamonds; these are the former animistic tribes whose lifestyles have been transformed by the Saviour's love.

Jewels that will last for all eternity are working in these mountains and forests to bring glory to the Creator and spread the message of salvation to the indigenous tribes. Gordon is the facilitator for the Christian message in Ratanakiri and he works closely with the Verners, Paul and Barnabas and the EFC. As he replants the trees of the forests, and cares for the animals God has created in this part of the country, he can hear the musical kongs ringing out through the valleys and over the hills as they are being used in worship and praise to our great heavenly Father whose plans for the good of these people are coming to fruition in the time he allocated for their blessing. This beautiful country that for such a long period of time has been under Satan's control, is now experiencing blessings from the King of kings who had plans for this land thousands of years ago. The people of Cambodia are precious jewels in the sight of God and many now shine for him in the place that was formerly the deepest darkness.

Gordon is able to teach and help the indigenous tribes to mature in the faith because he listened to God's voice and obeyed his instructions. The six months of waiting enabled him to become a member of Barnabas' house church. He also met the Verners and came under the spiritual input of Jim and the intercessory prayer of Agnes and Boury. The small indigenous churches of Ratanakiri were 'orphan churches' until Barnabas began to visit them. He became a shepherd to the shepherds and has developed a deep love for each of the leaders. He is able to speak to the churches without having a controlling factor so they are able to grow in the faith, retaining their own cultural values.

The situation that arose in these churches when Jim was called to help was so serious it could have wiped out the whole work. With Jim's insight, and the prayer support of Agnes and Boury, the churches were saved and reignited in their zeal for the Lord. Receiving spiritual food from Barnabas and Jim, Gordon has been able to minister to these churches now in a way he never dreamt would be possible. Jim had confidence in Gordon to such an extent that he passed on the mantle that Leslie Brierley had placed on Jim 40 years ago. When Jim laid hands on Gordon to continue this work, he felt a special anointing of the Holy Spirit that is enabling him to take a very different role in the church now, from the one he used in his early years in Cambodia. The believers basically have felt they own the work and they see Christ in them working their area for him. The work is self-supporting, self-propagating and self-governing.

Cambodia still needs our prayer support and more helpers to rebuild their society and the growing church. Great strides have been made but there is a long way to go.

To help the future generation to become godly leaders Brian Maher has a Diamond Project to train youth pastors, youth leaders, and other key young people from all church denominations throughout Cambodia to be better equipped with biblical knowledge, ministry skills and growth in godly character so that they are more able to lead young people in their churches and associated ministries.

The Diamond Project

The Diamond Project has an interesting history which is very appropriate for this book. A few years ago when the EFC Youth Commission was leading a seminar among the tribal peoples of Ratanakiri, Brian Maher and his co-director Seila were visiting a far-off waterfall when Seila picked up a pebble that was covered in some sort of crusty gum. He absent-mindedly began to scrape off the gummy substance when Revd Heng Cheng who was on the walk with them asked, 'Do you know what you have there?' Seila replied, 'Just a strange looking pebble.' Heng Cheng told him: 'It's more than just a strange looking stone. It's a gem.' Seila was dubious. 'You mean this dirty little stone? I don't think so.' Heng Cheng took the stone from Seila and pocketed it. Later when they reached the provincial capital of Ban Lung, they wandered around doing what tourists do, and stumbled across a jeweller who confirmed that it was indeed a gem. The jeweller polished it up a bit and they all began to see the potential of this gem. It was through this encounter that Seila came up with the name, 'Kamvetee Reaksmy Pek' which translated means the Glittering Gem which led to the Diamond Project.

Seila watched the jeweller refracting the sunlight, creating an inspiring image, and in his mind, he began to compare the process to Cambodian Christian youth, who are often overlooked and undervalued in their homes and churches, as being too young and inexperienced to be of any real service. He remembered his recent experience with the gem, picking at the crusty gummy parts of the stone. He did not recognise the value of the stone until Heng Cheng, an older and wiser man, pointed the fact out to him. Then when the jeweller began to work, Seila could see that each face of the rock needed cutting and polishing. He thought of the many Christian young people in churches and outside whose potential was as yet unrecognised and unrealised. Not many could see the value beneath the ordinary-looking layers. Many of these Christian young people were taught the Bible in their churches, and he compared that to cutting and polishing just one facet. It dawned on him that we needed to be cutting and polishing all the facets, spiritual, physical, mental and social. What other facets of Cambodian Christian youth needed shaping? – field work that contained ministry and exposure to orphans and young people sold into the sex trade – this was needed to teach them to follow Jesus' example and learn compassion.

In Khmer culture there was little idea of mentoring, therefore true discipleship was generally lacking in the evangelical church. So mentoring, practical skills, and other facilities were all added to the spiritual jewellers shop to shape the youth of Cambodia for a brighter tomorrow. The course is proving to be effective in helping the young church to put down roots in biblical teaching. It also teaches character building and stresses the need for the life of a leader to have a close communion with God.

The needs in prayer for this country are primarily for justice. There is no justice in Cambodia, especially for the poor. Generals use their troops to claim valuable land that has belonged to tribal groups for centuries. Many poor are displaced as the rich simply claim the land of the poor with bogus or forged titles. Decisions are made in favour of those with money who are able to pay bribes, and these decisions are upheld by corrupt judges in a corrupt judiciary system. Poor families cannot send children to school for lack of money, and those that do eventually drop out as they cannot afford to pay bribes to teachers for test answers. Brian has a burning passion to change these things by Cambodian Christian young people becoming professionals and influencing the system from within. He is also passionate about helping Cambodian youth translate their faith into works with the vision to rebuild Cambodian society. The Cambodian church needs a voice in the process of the rebuilding of the Cambodian society or it will repeat the mistakes of the past.

De-mining is still essential and Marie, the jeweller, has recently been on a two-day trip with her church into an area that has only been liberated from the Khmer Rouge since 1999. Their lives are difficult and most families are living on the edge of minefields. This land is free or cheap so families are moving into this dangerous area to claim the land. Some of the village settlements are cordoned off, so that only a small path through the village is mine free. Children need to be watched all the time and this is not possible as the parents have to work hard. There are still 60 to 90 live ordnance accidents per month.

Working in her shop in Siem Reap and networking with local communities, businesses and producers there are many opportunities for meeting people from all walks of life. Marie has been working with a group of amputee war veterans and demobilised soldiers in a literacy class and has set up a small micro business to enable them to make a living. This work has opened up the opportunity to set up a Sunday school for their children where they learn Bible stories and sing praise songs. Gradually their parents are coming along as well.

Marie says the Spirit of the Lord goes ahead of her opening up the way, inspiring and supporting her as she follows his directions. The proclamation of the good news is not only in words but through our lives, attitudes, activities and services, through our love for the poor. Her priority is to transmit faith in Christ Jesus, a faith that Christ proclaimed through his life unto the point of death and then to the resurrection and ascension.

Nigel Goddard is currently training development workers in a local non-governmental organisation. He has many opportunities of sharing his faith with Cambodians who do not know Christ. During a recent visit to the UK we had a good time of fellowship together with Milet and their two children. He sees Cambodia as a land of incredible contrasts, with half the population under the age of eighteen; still no education available to some of these young people who will be part of the Cambodia of tomorrow. It is a country of great beauty and serenity, yet only one generation ago it experienced one of the most evil and destructive genocides that humanity has known, with a third of the population dying at the hands of their own countrymen. This still has far-reaching effects in having robbed the entire nation of family and parenthood models; ensuring that the legacy of trauma could extend beyond the generation that experienced the Killing Fields.

However in this country where poverty, history and injustice have conspired so effectively to snuff out hope, here is also the setting for heroism, explosive church growth, of lives dedicated to the service of humankind. But above all the human activity that portrays the love and compassion of Christ, the great eternal God has plans for this country to yet become the 'Lighthouse for South East Asia'.

The candle shines so much brighter in the dark; so it is with hope, which blazes incredibly against a backdrop of hopelessness. There is good reason for hope as during the past ten years great strides have been made for a better future. Peace has replaced conflict, the Khmer Rouge have become a thing of the past, processes for reducing the size of the military force are in place; reforming the judicial system, introducing income tax, and a restructuring of the civil service: all these are taking faltering steps forward.

The Cambodian church has seen explosive growth over the past decade – from an underground church with the remaining survivors of Pol Pot's attempts to wipe out Christianity, to a vibrant bride that has a good level of freedom. It is only now that we can see one of the world's greatest tragedies and evils being used by God in his mighty redemptive purposes. The combination of a refining fire of a church that existed underground within a communist, anti-Christian regime, together with the witness of Christians who became Jesus' hands and feet, as they served the refugees practically and spiritually within the camps in Thailand, where hundreds of thousands of Khmer people fled to; the remarkable gift of evangelism that is inherent in the Cambodian church: all these strands have been used by God to build a church for a people needing to belong in a place, providing wholeness and unconditional love. The Khmer Rouge tried to steal every trace of love from Cambodia. Only God can restore lives that still carry emotional traumas, chronic levels of insomnia, and psychosomatic illnesses that are common in this land today.

There has been an outpouring of Christian support from around the world, through missionaries who are sensitive to the cultural needs of the people, and aware of the importance of the input of national leaders. It still needs help from international churches that are blind to denominationalism, that have humility and God-given wisdom to serve and support where support is most strategically needed. It needs missionaries who can see the strength of the local churches' evangelism, but have the grace to come alongside to encourage, nurture, disciple, and above all love the nationals as Christ loves the church. Cambodian church leaders are laying foundations through theological training and mentoring of emerging leaders who will take the Khmer church throughout and beyond this twenty-first century. They need the missions and non-governmental organisations that will stand beside them to bring kingdom values to the poor, the oppressed, the widows and orphans, the landmine victims and even those dying from AIDS.

And this is the hope, the future to be claimed for this young, energetic and maturing Cambodian church – to throw off the history of mistrust, rather than repeat it through disunity caused by denominationalism; to balance the incredible gift of evangelism with discipleship and leadership development. These are the challenges that the Cambodian church is rising to, often with the help, sometimes despite the help, of the wider international body of Christ, which has responded to the call to assist this new church to grow into the adult that I believe will yet be used to remind the western countries who have a Christian heritage, that they are in danger of losing their faith with lukewarmness, compromise, worldliness and lack of commitment.

As we attend our churches in the west, do we think of the needs there are in poor countries? Have we a heart of compassion for the poor, the widow and the oppressed? Do we give generously so that the incomparable message of salvation can be taken to those who as yet have not heard? These are not options if we seek to follow Christ and obey his teaching. Each one of us can play a part in seeing the kingdom of God spread so that finally we will hear him say, 'Behold I am coming soon! My reward is with me, and I will give to everyone according to what he has done' (Rev. 22:12).

There are countless Christians unknown to me who laid down their lives for the Lord in Cambodia. It is said that the blood of martyrs is the seedbed of the church. This relatively young church of Cambodia has a beauty and vibrancy about it that is beyond description. It has been my greatest privilege to worship with this church, to join in their songs of praise, and to watch with bated breath the amazing growth that has come out of their deepest suffering. On that final day those named in the pages of this story and countless others not known to me, will receive their crowns of glory for faithfulness to Christ. Many of them have become my closest and dearest friends. Their lives have been a source of constant inspiration and I believe they challenge us who live in the comfort of western civilisation to rise up from lethargy, shake off half-hearted commitment, get a fresh vision of Jesus in all his glory and follow him more closely so that we become like him. Then we shall be able to impact the next generation to rise up and fan the flickering flames of the sleeping western church into a fire that will burn so brightly it will challenge our decadent society and bring again revival to our land.

SAO Cambodia,
Bawtry Hall,
Bawtry,
Doncaster, DN10 6JH
Tel: 01302 714004
Email: admin@saocambodia.org
Web site: www.saocambodia.org